THE 5TH WORLD

MICHAEL ROTMAN

Michael J Rotman

The5thWorld.net

360-809-2582

Michael Spehr

360-804-2582

Copyright © 2012 Michael Rotman
All rights reserved.

ISBN: 1477580875
ISBN-13: 9781477580875
Library of Congress Control Number: 2012909972
CreateSpace Independent Publishing Platform,
North Charleston, South Carolina

CONTENTS

PART I ...and I awoke xiii

   Chapter 1 .... *1*
   Chapter 2 .... *9*
   Chapter 3 .... *19*
   Chapter 4 .... *29*
   Chpater 5 .... *37*
   Chapter 6 .... *51*
   Chapter 7 .... *61*
   Chapter 8 .... *69*
   Chapter 9 .... *87*
   Chapter 10 .... *99*
   Chapter 11 .... *111*
   Chapter 12 .... *121*

PART II   9/10 .... .129

PART III   The Material World of Angels .... .151

   The Material World of Angels *153*
   Level 1: Angels *157*
   Level 2: Archangels *161*
   Level 3: Cherubs *165*
   Level 4: Manners *167*

Level 5: Values... 169
Level 6: Principles...................................... 171
Level 7: Seraphim...................................... 173

PART IV   Worlds One through Twelve 177

World 1 183
World 2 187
World 3 195
World 4 201
World 5 205
World 6 209
World 7 213
World 8 215
World 9 219
World 10 221
World 11 223
World 12 227

PART V   Reincarnation 233

PART I

...AND I AWOKE

CHAPTER 1

HONK…and I awoke.

The sound seemed to hit my ear and then broke through, finding a place deep within my being. The sound of the horn opened my senses, as though I was sensing all of my favorite things in one moment. It was a new sensation. The sensation enabled me to perceive the world that I was experiencing in its wholeness.

What I saw was full of bright, then vivid colors. And I felt a subtle consciousness that gave me the sense of belonging, of substance and of purpose in this life.

After the initial effects from the sound of the horn had worn off, I kept walking in the direction of the park. I felt a little higher, and everything seemed a little lighter—as though a weight had been lifted off my back and put onto the world outside of me. I could feel the late summer wind around me, but the wind felt different than it had before—as if the wind blew with meaning. And as I walked to the park, I had a new feeling of connection to the material world around me.

I was relieved to get to the park. I felt that I had reached my destination successfully, and I could now relax a little. I just walked around the park, feeling its inherent beauty. After wandering around for about an hour in whatever direction I wanted to go, I felt satisfied and decided to go home.

As I walked home, I still had this new feeling of being alive and was beginning to gain a bit of confidence in the experience that had occurred earlier. When I got home, I didn't quite know what I should do with myself. I had all these new feelings and impulses to do new things. But I also saw my old habits staring me in the face.

I was conflicted with what I should do. It ended up that I decided to do the same things that I did before the experience with the car's horn, except now I would put a new twist on my daily routine.

...and I awoke

I did what I would habitually do. But I found myself continually trying to add some new expression to the habit to make it new. I would make an extra effort or say an extra word, with an attempt to fit my new feelings into the world where my old feelings were so ingrained.

If I was rejected or not understood when I made the extra effort, I would react by simply moving on to the next opportunity. But some, like my friends, would not let me go quite that easily. They would continue to inquire about my actions or words. But at the time it felt as though I had no answers that would satisfy them.

I was just living with the most liberating feeling that I had known to date. I didn't know that I had to answer to anyone for feeling free and feeling so good. And I didn't know that others had the right to question me on doing what I wanted to do: feel good and feel free.

I tried very hard to find the answers. Since the people questioning me had been my friends for years, the attempt to find answers to the questions on my mind was becoming impossible. But once a question was asked by someone, I felt an obligation to find the answer.

I was lucky that the first semester of my senior year was beginning to give me a solid distraction. It gave me things to do to keep my mind off the untamable desire to answer the questions on my mind. So as a goal of mine, I decided that I would take all the chaotic energy that was around me and focus it on creating a functional work ethic.

I spent my days right before classes just wandering around campus looking at all the new faces. I didn't want to be a part of anything or anyone at the time. Since I had my hands full, dealing with my relationships with my friends and my school work, and since my plate was full of important issues, I was able to walk through campus, connecting with anyone that I wanted to. I believed that it was some sort of serious game in which the connections created my existence. Even more than that, the connections were meant to happen by some higher force. It was a way for me to find new limits to what was, to me, a new reality.

I must have connected with hundreds of people during those days by making eye contact, saying hello to them, or even simply by sharing space and time with them. With each of these connections and the experiences that went with them, I was creating the world that I was going to live in.

Most of the time I walked around feeling as though I was living in a different world than everyone else. Along with the momentary connections to people, there were even momentary connections to buildings that seemed to have a character of their own. I related to the buildings and the trees as I walked by them since I felt comfortable seeing the same trees and buildings. I felt or thought that they couldn't hurt me with their rejections or question me for answers.

I think I just liked having things to connect to that weren't going to move. The next day they were going to be in the same place. And I could feed off of that reality and truth. It gave me the ability to believe that I was going to be there tomorrow and the next day, just like the buildings and the trees.

I continued my life in the way that one continues to age, and I went to the first days of classes. I sat and listened to teachers talk, and I did the homework that felt right to do. In creating my work ethic, I worked very hard towards the things that truly interested me. I realized that I was locked into my major, but at least I had my electives to spice things up. I took one elective because it had a great name—it was called Mind and Knowledge. I didn't really fit into Western philosophy well enough at the time to get from or give anything to that class. Then there was my other elective, Buddhism.

This class was only taught once a year and mainly for seniors, so my friends and I were excited just to have gotten into the class. In the beginning I could not have felt more out of my league. All I saw were the hungry eyes of philosophy majors and a teacher who was held in high esteem. I had never thought of myself as an intellectual, and I was honestly quite intimidated.

When my desires for the past, before the awakening experience, started to bubble to the surface, I decided to try out for the school's club soccer team. I had played and started for the team my freshman year, but an illness kept me off the field for a couple years.

Soccer had been one constant thing that I loved throughout my childhood. With hopes that my new

...and I awoke

feelings would fit right into something I had loved for so long, I ran for miles around the park with the team at practices and ran drills that were second nature to me. Everything was going well enough to put a smile on my face. Then the coach gave me an ultimatum. He told me to cut my hair if I wanted to stay on the team. Either it was my distaste for bad authority figures or it was the sense that I was now an adult, but I felt if I was going to make a change to myself, it would be because I wanted to. Obviously I didn't play for the school's team that year.

I had pretty much found my limits to my new reality on campus, but now I was going to get a running start and test those limits. I went to the library and found a couple schools that I thought I would rather attend—ones where I believed I would have more freedom to express myself. I started telling people that I was dropping out of school with plans to go to another school to finish my education. I listened to what my friends had to say, but what they were saying wasn't getting through to me. The next thing to do was to inform my mother, and she put out my desire to go with one word, "no." I had arduously made it through three years successfully, and there was no reason for me not to complete my fourth and final year where I was. If I wanted my expressions to be accepted on a higher level in a school I would have to look into Master's programs.

That was the end of the stream of consciousness from the experience from the car's horn. It was time to grab a paddle and head for the mainstream.

CHAPTER 2

As for my life outside of school, it was always interesting. I would go to any new place and feel like the outsider that I was. And if I liked it, I would go back again. For some reason, once I was accepted at the place and had emotional attachments to it, I didn't want to be there anymore. I think it was because I enjoyed the adventure of the new experience. And I am sure that it was because of how much I valued my freedom.

I often found myself stuck in a situation. I tried to make the best of it by being as creative as I could with each new experience. The creativity made the stagnation of the situation feel more bearable. In these moments I just saw life as a challenge and at the time I was not one to turn down a good challenge.

When I was home, I found myself thinking a lot about that day on the corner with the car horn. The questions from that moment still stared at me with furious intensity. So I got one of my notebooks out and started writing. It felt good to see on paper the questions that cycled through my mind. I felt better seeing the answers and thoughts written down on paper. It gave a material existence to what was previously spiritual.

I couldn't make much sense of why I wasn't getting along with my friends like I used to. So I found myself alone quite often as I wrote in my notebook. One time that I fondly remember, I was going to the park and sitting down to write. It felt as though what I was writing was of such importance. I was distracted by a girl in her early twenties with a boy of about six. The inspiration to write a poem came over me.

Before that I had always written more scientific things, so I was a bit wary at first. I looked at the girl and felt a connection to her, and I started to write:

> *In her purple beauty she walked*
> *And as she laughed the child appeared.*

...and I awoke

I wrote more, but I have lost that page over the years. But I felt alive again when I wrote those words, and I didn't feel alone. I felt as though she or the universe was in some way connected to me. And I felt the warmth of the connection. I kept writing in the scientific style that I was accustomed to and came to the conclusion that what I had just experienced was art, in its purest form.

The girl's name was Jessica. I had known her from before. I felt a very strong attraction to her but one that I couldn't put my finger on. Maybe the attraction was because we grew up in the same town, some twelve hundred miles away. This girl's attention had been driving me crazy. But figuring out what the attraction was, was more important to me at the time.

The confusion from my relationship with Jessica was starting to affect my already strained relationships. I was getting frustrated with my relationship with my roommate, Matt. And I was becoming less interested with my relationship with Ali, the girl that I had been with for the past two years.

After experiencing art consciously for the first time, I went home, and my mood had seemed to change a little.

Thoughts about my situation were not as difficult to deal with since I had another experience that was a true, substantial expression of my new feelings. Having written it down on paper gave me something physical that I could look at whenever I wanted to, and it would never change.

All my relationships seemed troubled. I chose to emphasize the fact that I still had a good and valuable relationship with myself. Instead of wasting efforts on aggravating social endeavors, I figured that since I was only going to be in college once, I recommitted myself to make this experience as educational as possible. I took a good look at my life and went forward.

Before college most of my life had been centered in a pleasure-based Western world, and that was the kind of world that I had immersed myself in at college for my first three years. I felt that it was time to test the waters of knowledge and learning, or intellectualism. Of my classes, Buddhism ended up having the most to offer. This class inspired me to attempt to solidify the experience created by the car's horn.

Buddhism seemed to fall in my lap. I had found a world that contributed to a lifestyle that I found very interesting. This new world to me was unlike the one that I had lived in for so many years. With Buddhism I didn't focus on the here and now as the only way to live. I was able to keep the experience that I had and have the attitude that I might understand it, maybe not today or tomorrow or even next year. But if I wanted to understand it, someday I would. And this philosophy was very liberating for me.

For part of the class's credit, once a week we would spend about an hour meditating. I was taught how to meditate, although I had meditated before and it came quite naturally to me. My favorite lesson was on the practice of "letting go." Letting go is the theory that one should not grasp to things but should experience them and then let go of them. This theory enabled me to release any troublesome thoughts that were on my mind. I believed that if the thought was important, it would return to me at some other time, and I would deal with it then.

Not only was 'letting go' interesting to me but it was also the introduction of another Buddhist theory. We read about three different kinds of enlightenment. There was the enlightenment of a disciple, which didn't fit me. There was the enlightenment of the Buddha, which also didn't fit me comfortably. Then there was an enlightenment that was defined to be "knowledge and illumination which, after being obtained without a teacher, is not imparted to any disciple."

It took me a few moments to make sense of it, and then I felt very comfortable with accepting this form of enlightenment as a temporary way to solidify my experience with the car's horn. I had taken hold of such labels as being Jewish and possibly being born again to help me during the early days of extreme chaos. But now with the acceptance of an Eastern world theory like enlightenment I could feel myself settling into the experience. It made me feel as though I didn't have to question the experience anymore but simply accept that it was. And with that consciousness I had found a good-sized piece of inner peace.

I was now able to give more of myself to the new world that I was living in. I had a label for my experience with the car's horn and a solid ground to educate myself from. With

...and I awoke

this newly found comfort, I decided to test the waters of friendship again.

These new friends showed me a whole new way of treating other people that was acceptable. I never would have thought it to be true if it weren't for the time that I spent with them.

In a way it was another culture to me, and at that time I felt as though I had only been accustomed to one kind of culture. I learned that treating people differently does not mean that you are treating them badly. In the culture that I grew up with, everyone pretty much treated people the same. If someone treated someone else differently, it was usually seen as bad or wrong and eventually the person conformed or became an outcast.

But these people, my new friends, did what they had to or wanted to do. If someone got hurt along the way, it was no big deal and it was ideally handled maturely. I didn't completely agree with everything that they did, but I realized that there was a way of living that was different from what I had known. I learned that there were some things that were different about them that I thought were bad.

And there were some things about them that I thought were good, and I really needed something good in my life.

With this new mindset, I felt I was a genuine outsider in my own life, and that was who I was. For the rest of the semester, I wandered the city when I wasn't in class. Conventional relationships were not my first priority anymore, and life began to open itself up to me. People became people. They weren't friends or enemies, just people. If someone attracted me, I approached them. Not being very good at conversation, it was difficult for me to make my connections grow on a personal level.

I felt like the wind, and if something got caught in my draft, then I made the best of it. Then I could walk away saying that I had met someone new. It was what I did to pass the time when I wasn't in class, and it slightly resembled a life.

Life seemed to matter in a way that I had never credited it with before. Life became something to cherish and enjoy on a personal level, instead of something that I ran through with my eyes half open to the things I wanted to see. My life actually seemed to matter.

...and I awoke

At the end of the semester, I decided to switch roommates from my friend of three and a half years to someone I had just met. With my new mentality to get me through the day, it was just a different person in a different place. Not being happy around my friends of years hurt a lot more than being ambivalent around someone I had just met. And ambivalence is a very underrated Eastern emotion.

As it was wintertime, and I had just made a relatively big move, I spent a lot of my free time on my commitment to creating a good work ethic. I went to classes and the library and did my work with the absentminded idea of graduating with everyone else.

I was given a reprieve after months of monotonous daily living. It was spring break, just long enough for me to go somewhere new that I had never been to before.

When I wanted to change colleges, there were two towns that I wanted to go to. The first was a town where a bunch of my friends from high school were attending college. And the second was a town that jumped off the page when I was looking for other schools. This town had a university that looked very interesting. It just seemed to fit very well into my life; I was meeting people from that town while in New Orleans. One time I went out with my roommate for a happy hour margarita and the bartender told me that I sounded like I had a 'Flagstaff laugh'. To be adventurous, I chose the second and decided to see my friends in the other town at some time later.

CHAPTER 3

After a long drive, I finally arrived in the town of Flagstaff. Being excited and relatively clueless at the same time, I looked for anything that gave me a sense of familiarity. The one thing that I was sure of was that I was hungry. I drove through the town looking for something that looked appealing. I saw a sign that said "Philly Cheesesteaks." How could I go wrong with an Arizona version of the famous Philadelphia cheesesteak? Even if it were bad, it still would have been good enough.

I had lunch, and it did its job of filling me up. When I had gotten outside the restaurant and had taken a couple steps, the smell of incense filled the air. One of the pieces of information that brought me to my decision to go to

Flagstaff came from a lady who held Indian sweat lodges at her home, back in Philadelphia. She didn't really know much about the town, but she remembered something about an incense shop that was near the railroad tracks. After smelling the incense and picking my head up to see the railroad tracks right in front of me, I thought that the store I was standing outside of was as good of a place to start as any.

It was a small shop with mainly Eastern religious knick knacks. I walked around the shop for a moment or two, and the man from behind the counter asked if I needed any help. After looking around the store, I asked him what there was to do in the area. He brought up the idea of going to see a Native American reservation. And since that was something that had been on my mind for months, I said okay, and he gave me directions.

I drove for a little while, and slowly the scenery began to become quite unfamiliar and the directions slowly slipped out of my mind. I stopped at a general store to get directions again. When I stopped to get directions, some guy who had attracted my attention told me how to get to

…and I awoke

the Hopi reservation and told me who I should go and see when I got there.

When I got to the reservation, I found the man who I was told to find with relative ease. I waited in his kitchen with what seemed to be a thirty-five-year old Irish woman, since he was busy talking to someone else. It was my turn to talk to the old man, after the gentleman he was talking with was done and had left the house.

The old man, Mr. Banyacya, pleasantly asked me a couple questions about myself, which I did my best to answer. I felt a little on edge, and I was trying to take it all in. Then he asked me why I was there. I honestly didn't know why I was there. But I knew that I wanted to be there.

The only reason, to my knowledge, that I was there was because the storeowner offered me the idea. But after driving two hours through the desolate, beautiful desert, I had forgotten all about the storeowner as a reason for being there. I think I had forgotten just about everything except my name.

Again Mr. Banyacya asked me why I was there, and I started searching for something in my mind that could be useful. I thought of a book that I had just read, and out of my mouth came the word "shamanism." I asked him if I could meet a shaman, like a child asks his parents if he could go get an autograph from a famous athlete. Mr. Banyacya became interested and was more than happy to give me the information that I desired.

He told me that they didn't call themselves "shaman" but preferred the less mysterious label of "medicine men." He told me the names of two medicine men and the villages that they lived in. Then he gave me directions to the villages. With that, I felt satisfied with our conversation. I said thank you and left.

I felt as though I had gotten into something or somewhere that I wanted to get into and had been given permission to continue my journey. I went to the first medicine man's house. After looking me over and questioning me briefly, he invited me into his house. He was a man in his early forties or so, and together we went looking for his father-in-law who was also a medicine man in the village. Eventually we found him, surprisingly enough, at his house. The three of us went back to the younger medicine man's house again and sat down at the kitchen table.

I just started asking questions, while the younger medicine man, Emery, sat in his seat as though he was a volcano ready to erupt. The older man, Martin, sat in his chair seemingly content to observe. As Emery began to talk, Martin sat up in his seat like a hawk. Martin was paying attention to every word that Emery said to me. Emery explained about the world that they lived in culturally. I was interested in what was being said, and I tried to understand as much of it as I could. Then Emery started talking about something that not only interested me intellectually but also passionately.

He talked about how they were the oldest continuous culture in existence on the soil that is the United States of America. He told me that they had a nine-hundred-year-old prophecy that had been passed down over the years. He talked about how the planet was about to change into the next world of evolving existence.

After talking for a while, I told him that I wanted to drive around the reservation to see what else there was to see. He made me feel as though I was welcome to come back any time. Then he gave me a look, which was to say that he knew something that I wanted to know. He had very deep and powerful eyes, and with that intense connection, I walked out his door.

I spent a couple days and nights driving around the reservation. It was beautiful land, and the energy was so peaceful. Everyone was very nice to me. Later in the week, I met a woman who had some land with a cabin on it, and she said that if I wanted to, I could stay there for a while. I told her that I had to go back to school, but my summer was free, and that I could come and stay there for a while during the summer.

I left the reservation around lunchtime. I wasn't in a hurry to get back to college in New Orleans. I drove smaller roads that were either going south or east. After about twelve hours of driving, I crossed into Texas. I figured that I would see how far I could go before I got too tired.

A couple miles across the border, I got pulled over by a policeman for driving seventy-one miles per hour. The road's speed limit was seventy miles an hour during the

...and I awoke

day and sixty-five at night. I was exhausted, and I found the situation a little irritating. The officer asked me if he could look through my car. I just wanted to get the situation over with, so I said yes and got out of my car. The officer opened my trunk and threw my belongings around as though they were garbage. Then he opened the front passenger door and exclaimed something. All of the sudden, the life drained from my body, and I sat down on the roadside. As I sat there on the side of the road, my memory started to come back to me.

For a month or so before I left for Flagstaff, I was reading *The Teachings of Don Juan*, by Carlos Castaneda. Before I left for Flagstaff, I remembered an old bag of mushrooms that I had. I thought that if I wanted to have a spiritual experience with a shaman, I would need to have some strong drugs, just like Castaneda wrote about. So I brought the bag of mushrooms with me on the trip just in case.

It ended up that the Hopis didn't use mushrooms or peyote. They used tobacco for prayer. So when the police officer opened the front passenger door and made an exclamation, I remembered that I had mushrooms in the car. I realized that the officer had just found them, and I had a feeling that I might be in trouble.

I got arrested on a late Friday night. The judge wouldn't be able to see me until Monday morning. I spent the weekend in the Littlefield, Texas, jail. I was guilty, so it wasn't very hard to spend the weekend there. It was an honest mistake. On Monday my mother bailed me out from Philadelphia. And now I was much more excited to get back to New Orleans and do some safe things, like go to classes and finish up the semester so that I could graduate.

I drove back to college and went to my classes as though nothing had happened. I kept the experience to myself for the most part. When I looked at some of the people who I had met during the second semester, I didn't feel as much like an outsider anymore. I felt as though something that I wanted, that had been dammed up inside of me for a while, was sent free. It was a similar feeling that I had when I wrote my thoughts down on paper. It was inside of me, and then it came out as something real and tangible. Other people at school may not have felt that it was substantial. But those that I met on my spring break did.

...and I awoke

I soon learned that my work on creating a functional work ethic still had some way to go. I thought that academically I was keeping up with my requirements, but in the mail I found a letter from the university telling me I wasn't going to graduate at the end of the semester. To state the obvious, my second semester of my senior year ended in disappointment. Not to mention that I had to watch my closest friends—Ali, Kate, Matt, Alex, and Brad—leave New Orleans, not knowing if I would ever see any of them again in this life.

CHAPTER 4

With the school year over, I stored my belongings at the house of my Buddhist professor's teaching assistant. She made me feel comfortable that my things would be safe there, and I was very thankful.

Comparing the reservation to my situation at college, there was no upside for me in the college town. And there seemed to be no downside to the reservation. I went home to Philadelphia for a couple weeks to see my mom. Time flew by and I was getting ready to go back to the reservation. I drove cross-country, and I was there. I got to the reservation and stayed at Rena's house for the first couple of days. Rena was the woman that I met on the Hopi Reservation when I was there for spring break. She let me stay in her house since she was at her house in Flagstaff. I laid on her couch in her nice home for a few days. Her brother came by and gave me the key to the cabin on their piece of land.

It was a small cabin on a nice spread of land on the outskirts of the villages. I couldn't see another house in any direction. I was alone out there, and that was exactly what I wanted. It took me a couple of days to get used to living in the cabin, but I soon found the silent, open air to be very therapeutic. After all the havoc that I had gone through at the university over the past year, I was especially happy to have some peace and quiet.

I was truly living as down to the earth as possible. There was a propane tank for the stove to cook my meals. There was a kerosene lamp for light when the sun went down. There was a barrel of water for drinking, cooking, and cleaning. And there was an outhouse for the rest.

Every day I would wake a little while after the sun rose, and for the first few days, I would go to my car to find out what time it was. I did that so I had something regular to start my day with. Then, for exercise and a

...and I awoke

sense of belonging, I would go to the field behind the cabin and plant corn the way I was taught on my spring break. I would take a couple steps, dig a shallow hole, and put a handful of corn kernels in it. After a couple of hours of that, I would return to the cabin. I sat inside and read, wrote, or meditated as the sun would reach its peak and then began its descent.

The most irregular thing that I did with my boredom was to see how long I could go without eating. I'd usually make it until about three in the afternoon each day, when I could no longer distract or ignore my hunger. When it came to food, I mainly ate porridge of ground corn and water. Once it was heated, I put some tamari—which is strong soy sauce—on it, and I became quite fond of it. But my taste buds did long for a familiar taste, so sometimes I would treat myself to a jumbo hot dog and an orange juice from the village grocery.

One day as I was leaving the grocery in the village of Hotevilla, my stomach was full and I was happy, and I walked past an old Hopi woman. As I walked past her, she called me "Pahana." Perplexed, I just kept walking.

The 5th World

I couldn't speak their language, so I had no idea what she had just called me.

When I had came to the reservation during spring break a couple months before, Emery and Martin spoke to me about the Hopi Prophecy. They spoke about the change in worlds that we were going through. They said that we were moving from the Third World into the Fourth World, but they considered Zero to be a World too. They told me about the three white men that would bring three stone tablets together and then they would know the answers that they needed of how to save their culture.

Later I had read about Pahana. Pahana was their lost white brother that would come to them as their savior. I read and I listened. But I knew that I was still a twenty-two-year-old boy, who was just beginning to become a man.

On the reservation I also met the Mowa family. The oldest Mowa brother, Augustine Jr., was in training to become the next medicine man in their village, after Augustine Sr., his father. Augustine Sr. and I spent a lot of time playing around. Sometimes he really was just a big kid. When he got tired and I still wanted to play, he sent me over to one of his other sons, David.

One day during my spring break, Augustine Sr. asked me to give him a ride over to David's house. David lived on some of the nicest land that I had ever seen, truly God's country. When we got to David's house, he and his wife invited us in. David, Augustine Sr., and I sat at the kitchen table and spoke. As we spoke the house began to fill with a very intense light. One of David's children opened the front door, and I was seeing Arizona the way I saw New Orleans just moments after the awakening from the car's horn.

David let me stay on his land for the rest of my spring break. I spent time talking to him, his brother, and his father in the village of Shungopovi, and with his friend Manuel in Hotevilla. Once I got to the reservation in the summer, I was happy to continue the relationships that I had made during my spring break.

Before the old woman in Hotevilla had called me Pahana, the Mowa family invited me to partake in a ceremonial Hopi dance. Augustine Sr.'s house was a stone's throw from where the dance was held. Augustine Sr. and his wife made me feel very comfortable in their home with all of their family.

At the dance I watched a circle of elaborately dressed men called kachinas dance slowly in a circle. The rest of the details are a little fuzzy. I stood in the Arizona sun in the middle of June for hours, without food or water and with occasional breaks to sit and relax. As the afternoon went on, I remember either the kachinas or other Hopi people throwing food to the people that were watching the dance. I felt as though it would be better if I did not let myself want any of the material things that were being given away. As the sun started to set, the kachinas started throwing things in my direction, but it felt like a test. I stood my ground and wouldn't move. I didn't move as a piece of fruit flew just inches over my head. And I didn't move much as an orange hit me very close to my heart. After I got hit, I looked over my left shoulder and, with surprise, I saw Augustine Sr. and his wife smiling at me. And I felt that everything was all right.

...and I awoke

I went back to their house, and I had dinner with their whole family. After dinner, I thanked them for everything and headed back to the cabin to try and digest the day. Part of the digestion process was reading a story of how Kokopelli was created. It was a relief to find that the story of Kokopelli's creation and the experience that I had with the kachinas was very similar.

The rest of my month on Hopiland was spent working at the cabin, talking to a few people, and slowly starting to say my good-byes. I noticed that the Hopis were very disciplined with their work ethic. If an interaction was not easy and peaceful, then there was no interaction and no desire for an interaction. I used the last week of the month to decompress and prepare to leave the reservation at the end of the month.

As I left the reservation, I called my friend in the other college town that I could have gone to for my spring break. I told him where I was and that I wanted to come up to stay with him to at least see the institute where I was interested in finishing my bachelor's degree. Now it had become the place where I wanted to do my master's work. He said sure, and I was behind the wheel again. About twelve hours later, I got to Boulder and met my friend at his house. He was living with two of our other friends from high school, but one was away for the weekend. Since my friend wasn't in town, I got to sleep on a normal bed, which I hadn't done in about a month.

The next day I went to The Naropa Institute and walked around and even sat in on a class being held outside under a canopy. The school seemed nice, but I got the feeling that I had to be some kind of a prodigy to attend the master's program right after getting an undergraduate degree. I think the average age of the students in the master's program was about thirty-two. I left with a dream and hoped to make a reality of it later.

I went back to my friend's house, and we took a hike that seemed to give us an overview of the Rocky Mountains. After that, I left to give myself enough time to be back at college for the first day of summer classes.

CHAPTER 5

I drove back to New Orleans, and I had a couple of days to spare before my class started. The month on the reservation had left me with a pleasant feeling of liberation, and I enjoyed the feeling. I had not forgotten that I had made a promise to a friend to attend a spiritual workshop. I was a little tentative since I didn't know much more about it than that my studies in psychology would be helpful. The drive back to New Orleans was planned so that I would definitely be back in time for the summer class, and I wasn't going to stress out about the workshop.

The workshop started at about 5:00 p.m., and at about 4:00 p.m., I was in a rush hour traffic jam on the highway just outside of the city. I got to the hotel where the workshop was being held with fifteen minutes to spare, which was enough time to go back down to the first floor to the cash machine to pay for my admittance. For the next three days, I stayed at my friends' house, the friend who I had promised that I would attend the workshop.

The workshop was interesting but also a little uncomfortable. Maybe it was my age or my inexperience. At the end of the workshop, the person in charge asked each of us to stand in front of everyone and reveal something personal. There was this feeling inside of me that I really wanted to get up in front of everybody and talk, but I also didn't want to because I was still very nervous. I was horrible at speaking publicly, but when it was my turn, reluctantly I walked to the front of the room. When I opened my mouth, a stream of sadness poured from my being. I didn't even know that I was sad about anything. Barely coherent, I revealed what I believed to be the biggest problem in my life. I said that the source of my sadness was that I was able to see the true reality of every situation, but I didn't know what to do about it.

...and I awoke

After I spoke there was a break, and I walked out on the patio to get some fresh air. I was happy to relieve myself of some of the emotions that I had been holding inside ever since the experience of the car's horn. I stood there alone, thinking and trying to make sense of the catharsis that I just experienced.

I saw a man sitting at a table across the patio. He was looking at me, and I didn't feel scared or excited. I actually felt quite calmed when I was connected to him. I walked over to the table where he was sitting. I said hello to him, and he replied by asking me a powerful and direct question without any warning: "What are you going to do with the information?" I smiled and had a feeling that I knew. I told him that I didn't know, because at the time I consciously didn't know. I only felt that I knew. Then I walked away from the table with a feeling of empowerment. I felt pretty good about myself. But honestly, I was still at least a little hazy about everything that was going on. After a little aimless wandering, I found my friend and we decided to leave and get dinner.

The 5th World

The next day I told my friend that I had to look for a new place to live that was closer to campus. I went out alone that night and ran into one of my fraternity brothers. My fraternity brother told me that he was staying in a three-bedroom apartment down the road. I was familiar with the place, and he said that I could stay in one of the rooms if I wanted to. I was so happy to have things apparently just falling in my lap, and I gratefully accepted his offer.

I had a place to live and a day to spare until my final class started. I went over to the house where I had stored my stuff while I was gone, since I now had a place to put my things. The person who had given me permission to leave my belongings wasn't there. One of her roommates took me down to the garage. I went through my things, and at least half of my stuff was gone. I was infuriated and eventually, with anger brimming, I took whatever I wanted to and drove off.

With anger I drove back to the new place where I was staying and carried my things safely inside the apartment. I exhaled and was ready to focus on my required class. I bought the textbook and other things needed for the lab

...and I awoke

part of the class. It was a simple class, and since it was the only class that I was taking, the work was even easier.

The summer days were spent with ease. After waking up, I would go down to the pool and swim laps while I talked to the pool man. Then I would get dressed and spend my days on campus. I would pick up a quick bite to eat, and then I would go to class. After that, I would usually go to the library and do my class reading or the assigned lab work. Then I was free, to a certain extent, to do whatever I wanted to. I would go to the park or the athletic center, depending on my mood. Some late afternoons I would go to yoga classes.

This was my habitual day until, once again, I found out that I was not going to graduate. And if I didn't graduate, I would have had to stay enrolled at Tulane for the entire fall semester. That was unacceptable. I needed one more credit to graduate. I was mistaken in thinking that the lab counted as a credit. I needed one credit and an idea quick. I found out that I could do an independent study for one credit. I just needed a professor to monitor it. As I stepped out of the Philosophy Department office, I walked right into my Buddhist professor. He had just returned from hiking in the Himalayas. He said that he would help me out and sign off as the professor that I would do my independent study for. He just wanted me to pick a topic and write an eight to ten page paper on it.

The first half of the summer semester flew by with great ease. Now the second half was going to be tough. I started working double time on my school work. If that wasn't enough, the stress from my situation was starting to affect my relationship with my fraternity brother that was letting me live with him.

One day we went to get lunch, and on the way back to the apartment he, Rich, asked me how much I was going to give him toward rent. Just to feel something besides stress, I jokingly said, "nothing." Before I could do or say anything, he was going off the deep end. He ordered me to pull the car over, and he got out.

At the time, I had graduation and only graduation on my mind. Taking care of my fraternity brothers' emotional fit was not one of my top priorities. I drove around for a little while to let everything sink in and then went back to

...and I awoke

the apartment. When I got back to the apartment, there were no logical or rational attempts made to remedy the situation. Rich told me that he was going to see a movie and that he wanted me out by the time he got back.

I took my wet clothes out of the washer, and the rest of my things were outside waiting for me. I filled my car with all of my belongings. I went to a Laundromat and dried my clothes. Then I drove downtown to the movie theater where Rich said he was. When the movie was over, I saw him and tried to show him the respect and gratitude he deserved, so that maybe we could work things out or at least remain friendly. But he was having none of it. I drove off to an indoor parking lot, next to Tulane's campus, and slept there for the night.

I woke up the next morning. I went to class, then to the library to get my homework done. Once I finished my homework, I went to my yoga teacher's house. I had seen her on Sunday at the Hare Krishna Temple.

On Sunday, I tried to tell her that I wasn't going to be able to come to any more classes since I wanted to focus most of my time on graduating from college. But she wouldn't let me say no to her and begged me to come back for one more class. I couldn't say no to her, even though I wanted to. And I told her that I would come by.

I finished my homework and went to get my car. I drove to my yoga instructor's with all my belongings in my car, including a twenty-five-inch TV on the front passenger's seat. I got to her house, and instead of doing yoga, we just sat around and talked. After about an hour of hanging out and talking, the instructor told me that she had to take her daughter somewhere.

I heard what she said, but for some strange reason I didn't care, I just wanted to stay sitting in the chair. Maybe it was because of the stress that I was under and I was starting to crack, but I couldn't get up from the seat.

After she and her daughter had gone outside, and I could hear that she was getting a little upset. I got up and went to the front door. I was trying to get the instructor's attention so that I could tell her that I didn't want to come back to class anymore, which for some reason never came up during our hour of hanging out and talking. But she was very hysterical, and I wasn't able to get her attention.

...and I awoke

I thought maybe if I spoke louder than her, I would be able to get her attention. So I started screaming at her to ask me never to come back. It was all that I could think of. I screamed it two or three times and ended up frightening her neighbor, but I still wasn't able to get my yoga instructor's attention.

The neighbor told me that she had called the police and that they were on the way. With that news I calmly walked down the steps of the porch and walked across the street to where my car was and waited. The police car appeared, and I was still just waiting to talk this out with the help of the police officers. Then I heard one of the officers ask my instructor if she wanted to press charges: charges! She said nothing, but a male friend that had showed up was demanding to have the book thrown at me. The police officers turned to me and told me that I was under arrest.

I went downtown and spent the night in a holding cell. In the morning I called everyone in my family to post bail, but no one was at home. Before anything else, I was paraded in front of a judge. Some people said some things to him and were allowed to go free. I had no idea what to say when the judge called my name, and I was directed to go to the gym and wait. After a while I was brought to a cell. I stayed there for the night and the next day. Some time in the afternoon, I was brought into another holding cell, but this one was just outside the courtroom. After a little while of waiting in the holding cell, I was called out to the courtroom with about nine other people. We all sat down in a row with our hands and ankles cuffed.

As we were sitting and waiting, the man on the far left went into a seizure. The person next to him was screaming for help, but no one was there. I stood up with my hand and ankle cuffs and made my way over to him. His jaw was locked, and foolishly I tried to open his mouth so he didn't swallow his tongue. I could do nothing, so I went back to my seat. A couple seconds later, the man was flailing his arms and got one of his arms caught between the seats. If he didn't get help, there was a good chance that he would have snapped his arm. But still, nobody was coming to help him. So I stood up again. I walked over to him, removed his arm from being stuck between the chairs, and laid him down on the ground. Once I laid him down, he relaxed

...and I awoke

enough to make eye contact with me. With my eyes I tried to tell him that everything was going to be all right, and he slowly came out of his seizure. Just as he came out of his seizure, two police officers and two nurses swooped in.

I had an innate feeling that he was going to be okay, so I sat down. As they were working on the man, I became a little concerned about catching some disease from him when I foolishly tried to open his locked mouth with my bare hands. So I stood up and walked over to one of the nurses and asked if she could give me something to wash my hands. Hysterically, she said no. Then the officers started screaming at me to get back in my seat. I sat down, but I didn't feel right about it. I helped this man when the nurses and officers were nowhere to be found. I thought that at least I deserved the respect to get my hands cleaned for what I had done. So I stood up again and asked to get my hands cleaned.

The officer didn't like that. He grabbed me and started to push me back into the holding cell. My shoe got caught under the door, and he stopped to let me get my shoe out. Then he threw me in the holding cell and pushed me. I was mad, but what was I going to do? I was half his size and wearing hand and ankle cuffs. He threw me around the holding cell, and the other people in there just watched. Finally, he got me down on one knee and took a full-force swing right at my face. It was too obvious, so I ducked it. But then I knew that he wouldn't be satisfied until he hit me, and I raised my face and put it right in his strike zone. He hit me under the eye and it split open. Then his six-foot, six-inch partner wanted his turn. He held me by the throat in the corner of the holding cell, after throwing me around for awhile and reared back with his right hand to really do some damage. As he was getting ready to hit me, a beam of light came out of my left eye, the one that had just been punched open. From my left eye, the beam of light was pulled into his right eye, and his fist became an open hand that he began to lower.

Two female officers ran into the holding cell and told me to get down and stay down, so I did. The two officers that had just beat me, picked me up and brought me to the prison dentist to give me eleven stitches under my left eye. I spent another couple days in jail to let everything settle down.

...and I awoke

The next time I was brought in front of the judge, the judge suspended my original charge of criminal trespassing and told me that if I wanted to get out of jail, I would have to pay the officer that punched me in the face five hundred dollars, because he said that while I was being beat, the officer broke his watch.

I just wanted to get out of jail. I told them that I didn't have any money, but I would come back on Monday and pay the five hundred dollars. They said okay, and I was free to go. I got a cab ride back to my car and was beyond surprised to see it still there with everything inside untouched, including the TV in the front seat.

I collected myself and knew that I needed a place to stay so that I could finish my required work for graduation. I drove over to the Buddhist Temple because I felt that I would be able to stay there. During the first half of the semester, I did a retreat at the Buddhist Temple, so there was a degree of familiarity. When I got there, I asked if I could stay there for a week and finish my work for graduation from college. The people there huddled up and decided that I could stay if I made a mandatory contribution of twenty dollars a night. I said fine and began to unpack my car.

During the last week of the semester, I caught up with my missed work, and my independent study paper slowly but surely began to come together. I took and did well on my final exam, and I wrote a pretty good paper for my Buddhist professor. I ended up getting a B- in my psychology lab class, and I got a B on my independent study paper. This meant that I had graduated college.

CHAPTER 6

After finishing school I decided to do my own version of the "taking a year off after college" classic. In my version I drove through the United States of America. This idea first came from a couple of places including my desire to drive back out to the Southwest and my desire to go to every state in America. I didn't have to be anywhere on any time schedule; I was free to go wherever I wanted, whenever I wanted as long as I went to each state. And this opened my mind to more possibilities.

Going to the Southwest was like going to a home away from home. I felt comfortable going to the Southwest from Philadelphia. I was beginning to get the feeling of freedom to do as I pleased, which was a feeling that I had missed.

The 5th World

I hadn't felt like that since my stream of consciousness had been brought to a stop. I was starting to feel that I was picking up right where I had left off. And this time I had even fewer responsibilities.

I wanted to remain relatively familiar with where I was going, so I decided on the southern route to get to the Southwest. I stopped at Graceland in Memphis, where I took the tour, and then I went to the Ozark Mountains in Arkansas. From there I drove through much of Oklahoma, and then I stopped a few places in northern New Mexico, as well as northern Arizona. I was letting my newly freed intellect open to experience life in the moment and absorb some of the wonderful information that the region had to offer.

It was as if a new material world was opening up to me. In these towns I kept hearing of the New Age as a way of life. Before it had only been words and kinds of stores that I had walked around in. My mind was filled with new, creative ideas, and living my life was encouraged like a child taking his first steps. After a week or so, the ideas became so stimulating that thinking before I went to sleep was

...and I awoke

taken over by sleeping after I thought, and some mornings I woke up tired. Due to this natural discomfort, I chose to turn my car around and head back to the East Coast.

I stayed home for a couple weeks and got some good rest and good food. It was nice to slow down for a while. My mother had planned a trip to San Diego to take part in a workshop. She flew to Santa Fe and I drove. I wasn't afraid of flying or anything, I just liked to drive and I was planning on going somewhere after the workshop anyway. We spent a day walking around Santa Fe seeing the sights. The next day she flew to San Diego, and I drove there to meet her. We spent a weekend listening to a facilitator talk about Egyptian high alchemy. He had us meditate on energy and where we were sending it. I enjoyed the exercise of being aware of where my energy was going, and I enjoyed having someone there whose job it was to care about our experiences and answer our questions.

After the weekend was over, my mother flew home and I got back in my car and drove. I drove through countless Native American casinos, and then I got back to the

Hopi Reservation. I stopped there, feeling accepted by most of the people there. I spent a day or two there to collect myself. When you are on the road, it's good to make the most of anywhere that you can call home.

After a few days on the Hopi Reservation, I went to the Grand Canyon. I was loaded with all the gear needed for just about any hike. I had plans to hike down the North Rim in the morning, so I thought I would go into the nice restaurant and fill up before the next day's hike.

As I sat down at my table for dinner, the waiter mentioned that Martina Navratilova was sitting about two tables away from me. I ate my dinner or at least half of it and left the restaurant. I walked with my leftovers over to the gift shop. It was my mother's fiftieth birthday, and I wanted to get her a card. I found a card that I liked and brought it up to the register when I noticed Martina Navratilova standing there. I asked her to sign the card for my mom. I thought it would give my mother's fiftieth birthday card a little special something. Martina agreed to sign it and I was happy. I went back to my car and got ready to fall asleep.

...and I awoke

I woke up in the morning and off I went. I hiked one mile downhill, which took about six miles to do, and got to the campground where I had made plans to stay. I put up the tent, made dinner, and just waited for the night to come so I could go to sleep. I fell asleep, and in the middle of the night, through the mesh cone at the top of my tent, I saw the biggest and brightest moon that I have ever seen. It was the harvest moon, which really doesn't mean much to me since I'm not much of a farmer. But it was so bright that it woke me clear out of a dead sleep.

I ended up sleeping late the next day and wasn't really in the mood to hike any farther in the direction I was going. I packed up all my stuff and started the six-mile hike uphill back to my car. After getting past the halfway point, people started to warn me that if I went too fast uphill that I would get sick. And others starting to warn me that I'd better hurry up before it got too dark to see where I was going. Having been given two completely opposing pieces of advice, I had two choices. My first option was to stop where I was and have a miserable night of sleep on a rock. The second was to put my head down and follow the two voices I heard ahead of me whom, I assumed, were hiking back up to the rim. I chose option number two, to keep on going. I made it to the top and found my car, then I proceeded to get sick before I could fall asleep.

I woke up, and after having such a wonderful physical experience during the days before, I was thinking that maybe now would be a good time for a spiritual experience. I was in my car, and I headed north into Utah. I mainly drove on the scenic routes that took me past southern Utah and into an area that actually had green trees and grass. I had been driving most of the morning and early afternoon when I decided to put the map down and just drive whatever direction I wanted to.

If I wanted to take a left turn, I did. I found myself lost in Utah somewhere and just followed the route signs. If I wanted to go east, I went east. If I wanted to go north, I went north. It was as if I had entered another state of mind, in which nothing mattered except where I was at the moment. And I didn't even know where I was.

I was living in the moment in an unfamiliar place, and at times it frightened me, and at times I felt elated. If I wanted to stop for food, I did, and without all the thoughts that usually accompanied my decisions. I walked right into the restaurant, placed my order, and not another person disturbed my state of being. I felt a lot of attention on me when I was ordering my meal. When I was sitting at a table waiting, I felt empty and alone, but it was okay because I was empty and alone. Even though I did get agitated a little while I was eating alone, I stayed and finished my meal. When I was done, I got back into my car and went driving. I didn't want to drive around in circles anymore and felt as though I had found what I was looking for, so I looked at my map to find out where I was and how to get back east.

On my way back east, I stopped in Boulder. I did my laundry at a Laundromat and then called up a friend, Matt, who was still living there. It was nice to have clean clothes, and I didn't want to impose too much on him. We met for dinner, and afterwards he said I could stay at his place. I was grateful for him letting me stay at his place. I wanted to look at the school that had the master's programs again, and I wanted to spend some time with my friend—not to mention that I wanted to relax and get some well-needed rest. I stayed in Boulder for a couple of days, and after getting as much rest as I could, I made my way back east.

I was home for a couple of weeks, and I was noticing that things began to change for me. People who didn't know me were, at the least, startled by me, probably because I no longer looked like I was from the suburbs of Philadelphia. My stories and the things I said at first intrigued most of the people that I did know, but I always seemed find a limit of what was tolerable and continued to cross that line. I could have stopped what I was doing to appease my friends, like I did when I was in high school, but I wasn't that person anymore.

I was lucky to have one of my newer friends, Jen, around. It was as though she continually wanted me to cross the lines that we lived in through our grade school years, and then examine the experience. She enjoyed creating and analyzing situations as I did too, and she made it fun. I spent a lot of my time between road trips with Jen. The best thing about her was that I felt comfortable being

...and I awoke

around her, and, more importantly, she was comfortable being around me. We had been friends for about a year and a half. She was a very intellectual person, so we had plenty to talk about.

With some of my other free time, I would go to the club Brownies 23 East to hear a Grateful Dead cover band that played there every Thursday night.

After spending some weeks at home, I wanted to go somewhere new, so I called my friend in Colorado. My friend, Kevin, invited me to come out to Colorado again and give skiing a try. I brought him a couple cheesesteaks from our friend's deli as a thank you gift. And I ended up eating most of them myself. I spent about five days there and got out on the slopes twice. I still feel that humans are not meant to go down mountains that fast. And from that you can probably correctly assume how I fared on the slopes. I still haven't graduated from the bunny slope but it was fun. I thanked Kevin for the experience and all the liberties that I took. And I made my way through the snow-covered mountain roads back to a familiar part of civilization.

The 5th World

CHAPTER 7

I was home for the holidays, and preparations were being made for a vacation to Egypt with my mother and younger brother. The day before we left, my brother and I looked at each other in disbelief that the next day we were going to be in Egypt. It was a long flight that was all made worthwhile when we were preparing for the descent into Cairo International Airport. Probably and thankfully, the pilot went a little out of his way to make a circle over the Great Pyramids. The overview of the pyramids was honestly breathtaking. I felt like an adult looking down on a child's perfect little sandbox.

We got off the plane and met our tour guide. We landed right in the middle of Egypt during Ramadan. The

Egyptian people were on their best behavior. For those who do not know, Ramadan is the holy time of the year for Islamic people. The tour, which my mother chose, was a two-week tour of the sacred sites of Egypt.

One of the places that I really enjoyed was the step pyramid of Saqqara. The pyramid was large but not too large for me to be able to comprehend it, due to the simplistic nature of its design.

Saqqara was actually the first pyramid built in Egypt and most likely in the world. I also remember the beauty of Cairo's Egyptian Museum, where I saw King Tut's

...and I awoke

golden mask along with numerous other worthwhile artifacts.

As we were nearing the final stretch of the tour, we made our way back to Giza. We stayed at a five-star hotel that had a view of the pyramids from the patio. My brother and I felt very at home there. The next day, our group got to take camel rides up to the Giza plateau. I took a horse. That night, we were given the opportunity to go inside the Great Pyramid and see the chambers. There was a chamber at the bottom that was quite intense. I knew that there was an underground tunnel that was said to bring out any fear that you have. If you made it through the tunnel without letting your fears get the best of you, you were rewarded with an experience well under the pyramid, in a chamber of crystals. Sadly, I didn't have the opportunity to go down there, but I believe other people on the tour did.

After seeing the king's and queen's chambers, it was past my bedtime. I went back to the hotel room and went to sleep. The next day, we woke up and some people went around Giza until the evening came.

Our tour guide invited us to his building for an evening of celebration, where we could clearly watch fireworks explode all around the Sphinx and the pyramids from his rooftop. It was a great way to say good-bye to Egypt. The next day we said our good-byes to our tour guide and boarded the plane to go home.

Once returning home, I began to become comfortable with the routine that was evidently becoming my life. I would go on a vacation of sorts when I had plans or felt inspired to do so. It wasn't a bad existence. I enjoyed being on the road and in foreign countries. When I returned home, I enjoyed being at home that much more; everything felt fresh and new again.

For my birthday I went up to New York City, and my older brother showed me a good time. A couple weeks later, my mother and I went swimming with the dolphins in Key Largo and whale watching on a boat in the Dominican Republic Whale Sanctuary. It was a beautiful and stimulating experience. Swimming with the whales was one the best trips that I had ever been on.

...and I awoke

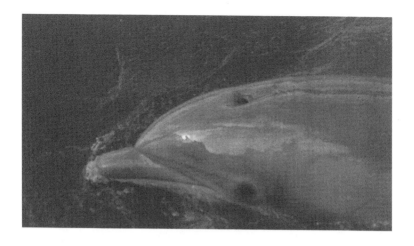

The trip was one week long. We returned home, and before the winter was over, I wanted to take one more road trip. I went to upstate New York to go through the Adirondacks. I spent one day in the mountains. I ate at a small-town restaurant and took the leftovers to the car in case I got hungry. I drove up a road and went as far as I comfortably could with my two-wheel-drive car. I stayed awake for hours writing in my journal, and then I went to sleep.

The next day I drove north past the Lake Placid ski jumps and caught an impressive glance of what they looked like. Then I crossed the border into the state of Vermont. I had one desire and that was to get some authentic Vermont maple syrup. It was a lot easier to find than I thought that it would be. It was starting to snow, and I was a little tired from staying up so late the night before. I pulled over at a mini-mart gas station and figured if I took a nap, when I woke up it wouldn't be snowing anymore. About two hours later, I woke up and the windshield and windows were still covered with snow. So I opened the car door to stretch and take a look: over a foot of snow in two hours. But the amazing thing was that it didn't seem to faze anyone there. I looked at the street: trucks and cars were driving through the foot of snow without any plows or problems. With excitement, I felt that if they could do it, so could I. I drove with traffic for hours, and eventually the plows cleared the streets and it became just another day.

I turned my car south and slowly made my way back to Pennsylvania. Around mid-April, with spring beginning to pop, I wanted to complete another chunk of one of my original goals, my goal to go to every state in the United States. I had already done a bunch of them with my father and my soccer teams as I was growing up. I was looking to the Northwest as the final goal, but before I got there, I had

...and I awoke

to pass through the northern Midwest. I decided to drive out there. I drove as far west as I wanted to, Minnesota, and worked back east from there. I started at The Mall of America and then went on my tour.

For about three days, I just drove and drove to get a feel for the state, and I even found one of the ten thousand lakes to go swimming in. When I was driving around Minnesota, I had the nicest feeling. The lake was definitely the highlight of Minnesota: clean, crisp water.

Then I crossed east into northern Wisconsin and looked at my map. I thought it would be funny to go to that little part of Michigan that sticks out of northeastern Wisconsin, the Upper Peninsula. It wasn't as funny as I thought it would be, but I did officially go to Michigan. Then I went back into Wisconsin and drove south. I saw some sights, like Lambeau Field, and went to some towns, like Madison. Then I decided to go home to rest, since I began to feel an inkling of boredom and tiredness.

CHAPTER 8

I was home and I left the door open as to when I was going to make my big trip out to the northwestern part of the country. The weather was nice, which made it easier to find comfort in my daily routine. Mainly, I caught up on my missed sleep, and I went to the park and listened to music as I walked around the fields.

One Sunday night in early June, my mother and I went to my grandmother's for dinner and had what seemed to be an average evening. It was nice to have the feeling of family around me, and that may have triggered something in me. When I got home, I laid down on the sofa and closed my eyes. I relaxed and thought for awhile. Then, as if my mind were jigsaw pieces to a puzzle, things just fell into place. When I opened my eyes, I was ready to pack my car and start my trip to the Northwest.

I decided that as soon as I had all of my things packed that I would go. A sleeping bag, a pillow, clothes for two months, cooking gear, food, a map, music and some money completed everything that I loaded my car with. I didn't think that I had forgotten anything, and away I went.

I started with South Dakota. If anyone is ever in South Dakota with some free time, seeing Mt. Rushmore is a must. I remember that the likeness of the presidents' faces was amazing. And the outstanding presence of the mountain-high busts carved and sculpted down to every detail was overwhelming. I stood in awe as I looked at the carvings until an overwhelming feeling of patriotism came over me, and after that I had to take a step back.

I went north to North Dakota and ran into a Native American sacred lake. I tried to listen to the Native

...and I awoke

American people there, but nothing that they said sank in. So I left the people and the lake and drove through North Dakota and into Montana. It was raining, but I can say that I got a good feel for the Big Sky Country. Driving the speed limit in Montana always puts a smile on my face.

Toward the end of Montana, I drifted down to Yellowstone National Park. I paid my park entrance fee, which at the time seemed to be a little excessive. I drove around the park feeling a little extra free, since I had paid for it. It was a good feeling of civilization in an area that was so uninhabited. There was a bit of a traffic jam due to a bear spotting, and soon enough we were moving again. Much farther down the road, traffic had slowed down again, but this time it was because of a bison walking on the side of the road. The bison crossed the street a couple of cars behind me. A bison walking freely: I wanted to get a closer look at this. I pulled my car over in a parking lot and grabbed my camera.

The 5th World

The bison came within ten feet of me without any reaction, at least any reaction that I could tell. I walked with him on the grass for about one hundred yards. Being that close to such a big, wild animal made me realize how futile so many of our fears are. It wasn't until I got back to the parking lot that I saw the sign saying that you are not allowed to walk on the grass.

I spent the night in the park at a campsite and finished reading Dante's "Divine Comedy." I enjoyed it, and the ending gave me a good feeling. The next day I drove south to the Grand Teton National Park. It was nice driving; the

...and I awoke

country and the mountains were beautiful, but my heart was still pounding from the action of the previous day. I turned around and went north, thinking that I might go back to Yellowstone National Park, but then I looked at my map and decided to go east.

I looked for one place that looked like the best place for me to go to in the remainder of the state of Wyoming. I decided on the one that sounded the best. Medicine Bow, Wyoming: now that sounded like a place that I wanted to go to. I spent two days driving on the groomed dirt roads during the day and spent the night watching the beautiful clear sky as the stars flashed with their incredible brilliance.

I woke up in the morning, and turned my car around, and thought that I would passively try to get out of Medicine Bow the way that I got in. I was trying to make good time, and I must have missed a turn because the next thing that I knew, I was driving over patches of snow that I had never seen before. I didn't want to slam on the brakes and chance losing control of the car, so I just held on to the steering wheel and let the car come to a stop on its own. It just so happened that my car came to a stop about fifty feet into a snow-covered road. The side of the hill blocked all sunlight, so all the snow hadn't melted by mid to late June.

I was grateful that the car didn't end up in the ravine. I tried to get myself out, but it became quite obvious: the only way I was getting out of there was by walking out. I grabbed my wallet and a bag of walnuts, locked the car, and started walking.

I guess I had walked about ten miles, during which I really think I saw water going uphill. Ten or fifteen miles into the walk, I saw a pickup truck. It was a father and son out watching the elk. They gave me a ride into town. I got a hotel room and some dinner and went to sleep.

In the morning I found out that I could get my car out the snow. I would have to wait for a while at a nearby bus stop, then I would take a bus to a relatively abandoned bus stop. After getting dropped off at the bus stop in the middle of what seemed to be nowhere at around midnight, I called a cab that was waiting for my call, and he took me to

…and I awoke

a motel. The motel owner knew that I was coming, and he left a room open for me.

The next morning I met up with the tow truck driver. He and I drove out to my car together. The tow truck driver got my car back onto dry land with relative ease. I got into my car, very happily, and started my drive out of Wyoming and into Idaho.

Miles and miles of wilderness were easy to come by. I went as far north as I wanted to go and ended up on a beach in Coeur d'Alene. Swimming and basking in the sun was just what I needed after being away from civilization for a few days. After a day at the beach, the evening was setting in and I went looking around for a place to have dinner.

Again I found a place that served Philly cheesesteaks, and I saw no need to search any further. I ordered my meal and ate it on their outdoor patio. When I was done, I thought of either going to a hotel for the night or to see what was going on inside the establishment. There was a band playing that wasn't very good, but good enough for someone who hadn't heard live music in awhile.

The 5th World

The band stopped playing, and I asked one of the guys in the band why. He said that the Tyson vs. Holyfield match was about to begin. They said that they would continue playing after the boxing match was over. I decided to sit and watch the fight. I had been watching Tyson's matches since the beginning of his career, and my friend Kevin from Colorado was a big, "real deal" Holyfield fan.

The boxing match was going like any other. Then Tyson bit Holyfield in the ear. I had never seen anything like that before. And before I could make any sense of it, Tyson did it again. This time Tyson actually bit off a piece of Holyfield's ear. Everything erupted in chaos, which continued for a little while. In the establishment that I was in, the chaos had died down and the band was getting ready to start up again.

I couldn't get into the music with all the thoughts running around in my head related to what I just saw. I decided to leave the bar and look for a place where I could freely think about what I just saw. I found a secluded clearing deep in the woods. I laid down and tried to work out all the thoughts that were in my head.

...and I awoke

Since my awakening, just less than two years prior, I had started believing in things like karma and reincarnation. And I knew that Holyfield was a good guy, but I couldn't understand why something like this would happen to him. Then some of the pieces in my head started to fit together. I came to the conclusion that Evander Holyfield was Vincent van Gogh in one of his past lives. Holyfield, having a part of his ear bitten off, was the truest definition of karma. With that conclusion, my mind was at peace enough to fall asleep.

I woke in the morning and found some dirt roads to drive through for most of the day. I had become accustomed to driving scenic routes and back roads. These back roads were probably roads used for business purposes, like logging. Besides all the rocks in the road, I found the closeness to nature on these logging roads to be incredibly pristine, maybe the cleanest energy that I had the pleasure of experiencing to date.

I was driving down a dirt road, and all of the sudden, a bear ran out in front of my car. I had seen all different kinds of animals on my journey, but this was the first bear that I had seen. I was not one of the people who saw the bear at Yellowstone. I stopped the car. By the time I had gotten out and ran to the front of my car, the bear was gone into the woods. I got back into my car and turned the ignition, but it wouldn't start. I tried again and again, but there was nothing. I had to use any trick that might work, since I was stuck in the middle of nowhere. I put on some Bob Marley music. So I knew the battery worked, and then I tried to give my car as much of my energy as I could. I turned the key and the car started.

Awhile down the road, I found civilization, which included a gas station, and out of habit I turned off the ignition to fill up the gas tank. When I got back in the car, it wouldn't start, but at least I was at a gas station this time. A gas station is a good place to be if your car ever breaks down. I asked the attendant if he could help me, and he said that he would take a look at it. We pushed the car into the garage. He said that the problem was the starter, and they didn't have a match in stock for my car. The attendant said I would have a better chance down the road at the next town, because they had an auto

...and I awoke

parts store. I said okay, and the attendant got the car started with some crafty under-the-hood workmanship. He warned me that if I turned off the ignition, the car wouldn't start again, unless I did what he did. And there was a good chance that I would get electrocuted if I did it incorrectly.

So I drove to the next town and was disappointed to find that the auto parts store didn't have what I needed. They told me that I would have to wait a couple days until the end of the holiday. Then I would be able to get a tow truck to take my car to the place that would have the part I needed.

I turned off the ignition, left the car outside the auto parts store, and walked into town. It took me about an hour to forget about the situation that I was in, and to start enjoying the carnival that they had set up for the holiday weekend. There were games and music and food stands. I had a lot of fun, considering my situation, and the evening was coming in so I went back to the car to sleep the day off.

The next day was more of the same. I played around at the carnival, where I had become comfortable. After the carnival, everyone started walking in the same direction. I asked someone were everyone was going. I was told, "the rodeo." So I went to my first rodeo. When the day was done, I was exhausted from all the excitement and I made my way back to my car. I called to confirm that the tow truck was going to be there in the morning, and I went to sleep.

Bright and early, the tow truck arrived, and I was delighted. We had to go pretty far to the place that had the part that I needed. Since it was a holiday, the driver decided to bring his wife along so they could spend some time together in the town that we were driving to.

My car was put up on the flatbed, and the driver told me that there wasn't enough room in the truck for me and that I would have to sit in my car on the flatbed. It seemed strange, but I had no choice, so I made the best of it. The battery in the car worked. So I sat back and listened to my 2-13-70 Grateful Dead tape as I stared out the window at the passing cars. And I did get some interesting reactions.

...and I awoke

Eventually we arrived at the garage that had the starter solenoid for my car.

I got out of the car, and the people there were trying their best not to laugh at me, as they had seen me sitting in the car on the flatbed. The car was unhooked, and I was standing there with only one thing on my mind: my new starter. The guys who worked at the garage told me that they had a barely used starter solenoid, and it would be inexpensive. But it wouldn't be there until the next day. By this point in time, I had gotten so used to being disappointed and having to wait. I took the news relatively in stride.

I went to the movies, and I talked the people that worked there into letting me see the movie a second time for free, so I could comfortably waste the time. After the movie I treated myself to a nice Chinese dinner and then slept well. The next day came, and the garage got the part I needed and assembled it without a hitch.

After Idaho I headed west into eastern Oregon. I let myself drive freely without a goal in mind to celebrate the fact that my car was fixed and I had a full tank of gas to drive with. On 7-9-97, I pulled into Ontario, Oregon, with a population of 9,700 people. I took a turn and saw Cairo Middle School and continued down the road. About a half mile past the school, I was just looking out my window, and across the street there was a wheat field with a crop formation in it.

It wasn't one of those intricate, sacred geometrical shapes. It was just formations. Within the formation was matted, woven wheat. I grabbed my camera and a pen and paper and got out of the car.

...and I awoke

I had just parked my car on the side of the road. I crossed the street in a state of awe. I didn't want to trespass on anyone's land, so I walked along the road in continual awe. I saw a woman in her garden outside of her house. I politely introduced myself, and she asked if I had had any breakfast. Surprised, I said no. She said that I could eat as much as I could pick. She said this as we were surrounded by her raspberry vines.

As I picked and ate raspberries, I asked her about the wheat fields. She said that she knew nothing about it, but if I wanted to, I could look around for myself. After a few more fresh raspberries, I took her up on her offer. I walked along the wheat that was hers and was blown away by what I saw. It was so stimulating that I was having difficulties focusing on one thing at a time.

After studying one formation in particular for a while, I was exhausted, and I needed some lunch. I went to the general store near the middle school, and the cashier told me that there had been a huge electrical storm that came through town the night before. He said that there were formations all over town.

I went and saw a few of the formations after I had lunch. Then I drove back to where I started. I parked my car in the same spot as before. And with my pen, paper, and camera, I walked right into the formation and sat down. I tried meditating, writing, lying down, and taking pictures. Anything to try and fully connect with the energy that I was feeling. As I sat there, I began to feel the energy of the crop formation for what it was worth.

The energy was similar to the energy of swimming with the dolphins. But it was also similar to slowly walking around the fourth floor of The Museum of Modern Art in New York City. The energy was very intellectual, but also light, pure, and natural. I think I stayed there just long enough to take a piece of it with me for the rest of my life. By the end of the day, I was exhausted. There was a scenic lookout about ten miles down the road. And that made for a perfect place to sleep that night. Before I fell asleep, I basked in the feeling of becoming a successful journeyman.

In the morning I drove north, and after driving past Mount Hood, I ended up at the Mount St. Helens National

...and I awoke

Volcanic Monument. The site overlooked the volcano from a distance, and a woman held a class explaining the eruption and the devastation of it. After the class I stayed there for a little while and then got back into my car with the idea of seeing Mount Rainier. I drove farther north. When I got to Mount Rainier, the fog was so thick that I couldn't see the mountain. Disappointed, I drove on to Seattle. On my way to Seattle, and as I was merging onto the highway, I looked in my rearview mirror to see if there was any oncoming traffic. In the mirror I caught a crystal-clear glimpse of Mount Rainier, and it was awesome.

Not knowing my way around Seattle, I just drove around until I found a place that I liked. I parked and got out of my car. I went into the aquarium, and I took a walk at a nearby park. I went on to an outdoor market and walked around the stores in town. I wanted to do something fun that night since I was in a big city. I decided to go and see a baseball game. I had a seat in the left field bleachers and enjoyed the game very much. The next day I decided to go south along the West Coast.

CHAPTER 9

On my way south from Washington, I stopped in a small town in Oregon that had a cute little boardwalk with stores full of candy and games. I went off the boardwalk and down to the beach to stand by the ocean's edge. As I stood on the shore, Jessica popped into my mind. It had been nearly two years since Jessica had become an enigma to me. And on this day, she was still as much of a source of confusion as ever. After thinking about her for a minute or two, I turned around and saw some people playing beach volleyball. I had to give it a try. I asked to play, and we ended up playing until the sun went down.

The next day I headed down the west coast of Oregon. For years I had wanted to go to Eugene, so that was my plan. I walked around Eugene during the summer, and it really wasn't that interesting. I got back in my car and found the on-ramp to the I-5 South. As I got on the ramp, I felt my energy being pulled down, similar to what happened at my yoga instructor's house. This time I tried to get away from the feeling, since it didn't work out very well the first time when I remained seated. I floored the gas and was going pretty fast as I was planning on merging with traffic. Then I heard the sirens and saw the flashing lights. I got a speeding ticket on the on-ramp.

After getting the ticket, I was mad and I didn't want to drive on the highway anymore. I pulled off the highway as soon as I could and decided to do the opposite of whatever I had planned. Maybe that would change my luck. I drove around and stopped and asked the first people that I saw. Back then, I had a long, unkempt beard, and my hair had become one big dreadlock, sprinkled with the sand from the Sahara. So when people saw me, they thought I was interested in hippie-type activities. So when I asked the first people that I saw what I should do while I was out there, I shouldn't have been surprised

...and I awoke

when they told me to check out a place that hippies went to near Bend.

It sounded like an adventure, so I said thank you and started driving east. After driving for about an hour, I saw a couple of cars and people on the side of the road. I gently pulled my car over and approached them. I don't think I said much more than hi, and they asked me if I wanted to come in their house. Inside the house, most of the people were getting ready to go somewhere. I asked where they were going. And I was told that they were going to Cougar Hot Springs. I said that I didn't know how to get there. And one of the guys in charge said that he would go with me in my car, since he knew how to get there.

The first place that we stopped was the hot springs. The water was warm, not hot, but they were still happy to jump off the rocks into the water. Then we packed up and kept driving down the road. Farther down the road, it came to a dead end. But before the dead end, there was a line of cars parked on the side of the road. I parked my car near the dead end and started walking around. There were people talking, smoking, hanging out, and playing hacky sack. Or at least that was what I saw.

I must have played hacky sack for hours, because when I looked up, it was getting dark. The guys that I was playing with explained to me that the nickname for the road that we were on was 4:20. They said that I could cross the bridge and take a right into Hippie Hallows. Or I could take a left and go to Hippie Heights. It sounded right to take a right into Hippie Hallows.

I walked back up 4:20, and people were already beginning to leave. I got into my car and drove down the road and across the bridge. I took the right turn after the bridge and drove until I found a nice place to park my car. I ended up parking my car right next to another car with Pennsylvania plates.

I got out of the car and slowly wandered up the dirt road. At the top of the road on the left was a big communal kitchen, and on the right was the beginning of a huge drum circle around a bonfire. I stopped at the kitchen, and they were happy to give me food, but I could feel that they wanted more from me than what I was happy to give. But

...and I awoke

since the first one was free, I ate dinner as I meandered around the bonfire being made. After I ate, I thought about going to my car to get my drum, but again I felt a strange, uncomfortable feeling. So I didn't. But I did sit down and play some drums for what turned out to be a really good time.

As some people were still playing, I was exhausted and went back to my car to get some sleep. I woke up in the morning and noticed that the girls from Pennsylvania had left. I decided to move on to Hippie Heights. I drove up the dirt road till I crossed the bridge, then I drove down to Hippie Heights. I found a place to stay, but I wasn't happy with it because I felt like I was on a stage—a stage that angled downhill. So across the dirt road and up against the river's shore, I found a soft, flat, grassy area that was perfect.

I first thing I did was set up my camp. I made my tent. Then I hard-boiled some eggs to eat. After I ate I felt good and started walking around. There was a bus full of people that were the closest people to me. After meeting them and listening to some of them play music, I kept walking.

I found a guy that had a puppy named Nesta, Bob Marley's middle name.

After playing with the puppy for a while, I returned to my camp. When I got back to camp, I noticed that the car from Pennsylvania was right next to me. That night I could have gone back to Hippie Hallows for the drum circle, but we decided to have our own. I stayed at Hippie Heights for about five days. I met all kinds of people: people there to drink around a fire, people there to do yoga by the waterside. Instead of going into stories in which the details have become fuzzy over the years, I will simply say: for as horrible as the five days in jail in New Orleans were, the five days at Cougar Hot Springs were equally incredible. Well, almost.

After the hot springs, I drove southwest into Northern California. My first stop was Mount Shasta. Besides the mountain, there was a nice, quaint little town. I spent the day walking around the town and went into a couple shops. I decided to check out the mountain, so I got in my car and started the drive upward. The farthest place I could go was a campground that seemed to be about two-thirds of the way up the mountain. I parked my car and wandered around the campground for a little while. Then I got in my car and got ready to go to sleep. The energy was very light and stimulating, unlike any other place that I had ever been. It had a strong feeling of excitation, as if it were about to explode.

I woke in the morning to the sound of someone screaming, "Happy birthday, Jerry." There was a concert that most people were going to, but it seemed that if they could, they would have rather been in San Francisco. Nothing was stopping me, so I decided to go down to San Francisco for the anniversary of Jerry Garcia's birthday.

On my way to San Francisco, I thought that I would like to see the redwood forest. I had been to the redwood forest when I was younger, and I remembered it to be amazing. I drove toward Eureka, which was southwest. I got to the forest and drove through it.

After driving for a while, I pulled over to a place where I could get out of my car and look around. The trees were still amazing. There was someone else at the turnoff. His car had an Arizona plate on it. As I approached him, he offered me a piece of fruit. I said sure and then was in a hurry to get back to my car and down to San Francisco. For some reason, the person really stuck in my mind. I couldn't stop thinking about him. And when I thought about him, I thought about the person who was talking to Thomas Banyacya before me at the Hopi Reservation.

As I drove through Northern California, I was trying to figure out who the person that I had just met was. I felt that this person that I had just met in the redwood forest and the person who was talking to Mr. Banyacya about making a movie about the Hopis were in some way connected. I kept remembering things that Emery had said about three stone tablets being the answer to the Hopi Prophecy.

I continued thinking about how these two guys were not substantial enough to make anything happen. Then I thought about my two brothers. And the substance was there, but I couldn't ignore the other two guys. I decided that prophecy is an art form before it becomes a science, and before it becomes a fact. I felt that this prophecy was not entirely ready to be realized yet. I believed that as the

...and I awoke

pieces fell into place, the prophecy would be realized, but not until the pieces fit together just right.

The next thing that I knew, it was dark and I was looking at the Pacific Ocean from a parking lot in San Francisco. I got out of the car and started walking toward a bunch of people sitting around a fire on the beach. As I got closer, they broke into a rendition of "Happy Birthday." I laid by the fire for a while, then went back to my car and feel asleep.

I woke up in the morning, and there was a parking ticket on my windshield. The officer let me sleep but still gave me a ticket. Once I woke up, I found out that the Furthur Festival was at the Shoreline Amphitheatre. I had never seen a show at the Shoreline Amphitheater, so off I went. The day was a marathon of music. When the music stopped, I left the amphitheatre and went looking for my car. I found it, got in it, and went to sleep.

I woke up in the morning and remembered how much I enjoyed being in Berkeley when I was a child. I drove out to Berkeley and went straight to the shoe store. When I was at the Cougar Hot Springs, I walked right out of my sneakers, and my sandals weren't the most comfortable shoes in the world. So my first stop in Berkeley was at the shoe store to get new sneakers. I was so excited to get new sneakers; I think I lost my wallet there.

After getting new shoes, I drove around looking for anything interesting, and I pulled over by the bay and washed my car. After the day of work, I decided to go back to San Francisco because I was looking for something to do that night. I found a small club on lower Haight Street that had a Grateful Dead tribute night.

When the night was coming to an end, I went toward the front door. I walked out of the club at the same time as some guy that I had noticed when I was dancing. He asked me if I could give him a ride home. And I jokingly said, "Sure, if I can sleep at your house." He said yes.

His name was Gabriel. He lived in Berkeley with his son and his son's mother. Gabriel made me feel at home during the couple of days that I stayed with him. Between him, his son, and I, we had a lot of fun. One game that I liked was making him Archangel Gabriel and myself Archangel Michael. When I played this game with him, it felt real.

...and I awoke

Eventually I had to move on. So I got in my car and said good-bye. I drove to Oakland for lunch. After lunch, I remembered that my step-sister lived in Oakland, and I gave her a call. She was happy to hear from me and drove over to where I was so she didn't have to worry about giving directions. She met me, and we went back to her apartment.

The next day we spent at the zoo and hanging out. My step-sister worked at a store on Haight Street in San Francisco. The next day I went with her to her workplace and met my friend from middle and high school, Chaim, there. We went back to his place, and it was just really nice to see him. The next day he went off to work, and I spent the day with another friend from grade school.

The day after that, Chaim had to go to work again, and I just went down to the street to see what I could find to do. I ended up finding someone that was going to a Renaissance fair, and he invited me along. I spent the day wandering around the fair as they were preparing to open. I got home later, and Chaim and I went over to my step-sister's apartment. When I was there, I was looking through my stuff, and I realized that I no longer had my wallet. I didn't keep my money in it, but it did have all my cards and phone numbers. I was searching for it because I had Jessica's address in it, and that was something I liked to have, almost like a security blanket.

When I saw that it was gone, instead of freaking out, I logically thought that I could call information for Jessica's father's number, and her father would give me her address. Now that I look back at it, I think my actions may be considered a bit obsessive.

I got her father's number and called to get her address. When I called I asked if Jessica was there, to my surprise her father said yes. She and I said hi to each other, and she said that she had to go. I told her that it was nice to hear her voice, and I hung up. Chaim and I went back to his place. Later that day it was time for me to go. I loaded my car up and left the Bay Area for Philadelphia.

CHAPTER 10

I got into my car and made a loose plan of what route I was going to take back to Philadelphia. I decided that I wanted to go through the Hopi Reservation and say good-bye to my friends there, since I didn't know when I would be returning.

I drove through Nevada, and while driving through Nevada I stopped at a McDonald's for lunch. I got my lunch and sat down at a table next to two men that were reading the Bible. After eating and cleaning up, I had to ask them more about themselves and what they were doing. They invited me to sit down with them. I confidently sat down since I considered myself someone who had studied a lot about religion: from Judaism to Buddhism, from Taoism to Confucianism and Hinduism.

The 5th World

We spoke quickly, and then one of the men asked me if I had accepted Jesus Christ in my heart. To my knowledge, I hadn't. Then the man asked me if I would like to accept Jesus Christ in my heart. With a feeling of obligation, the man said a few words, and I felt a warm feeling in my heart chakra. I said thank you and left that McDonald's in the middle of Nevada.

I drove to the reservation and said good-bye to my friends that were home. Then I continued the cross-country drive back to Philadelphia. As I got closer to Philadelphia, I was thinking about Jessica more and more. It was as though the thoughts of there being a possibility that I was going to see her once I got back to Philadelphia, in a way helped to motivate me to finish the drive. When I got off of Highway 76, I realized that I had to pass her neighborhood to get to my house. So I pulled over and called her father. He said that he would no longer help me to find his daughter. I respected his wishes, but I still found them to be a little strange.

I went over to a mutual friend's house and could tell when I approached the door that I wasn't going to get much help there either. I stayed there for an hour or so talking and catching up. After slowing down to talk with old friends, I realized how tired I was. And all I wanted to do was go home and sleep.

I was home, but I couldn't turn my switch off completely. Not after the great experiences and all the fun I had on my two-and-half-month tour of the northwestern United States. So I remained relatively active. I was seeing a bunch of concerts and trying to get whatever information about Jessica that I could.

I saw one of her friends driving, and I flagged her down. I asked her if she knew where Jessica was. She said that she was probably at her mother's and then gave me directions on how to get there. I drove over there and saw her gold Volvo parked in front of the house. I knocked on the door, but there was no answer. I went home and called information to get her phone number, and then I called and left a message on her mother's machine that I wanted to see her.

Either it was later that day or the next day, I got a phone call from my father about a written message that he found on his car. As he was explaining that Jessica had left a hysterical message, the other phone line in the house rang. My mother answered it because it was her line. All I could hear her say was, "No, if you have something to say to him, you have to tell him yourself." With that my mother handed me the phone. Jessica was trying to calm down, but she was still quite hysterical. She said something that was close to: never call me again, don't talk to my friends. I said okay and good-bye.

I may have been a little overzealous, but around that time I was very passionate about my life. I didn't feel that I was in the wrong; I just thought that Jessica didn't want to play with me anymore. So I went off and played with other people, like I was doing anyway.

I wanted to get out of Philadelphia, to process the Jessica episode, and I chose to spend some time with my brother in New York City. I got to New York and went up to his new apartment. He said that we were going shopping because he needed to buy a few things and thought that he could use my opinion. He quickly found a coffee table, then laboriously found an oriental rug to put under the

...and I awoke

table. Then we walked around Central Park, and he told me that he had something to do. We decided where and when we would meet back up.

I wandered around the park taking pictures. When it was time to meet up, I went to the place and my brother wasn't there yet. There was a cute little New Age store, so I walked in it. I found a box full of the coolest crayons that I had ever seen.

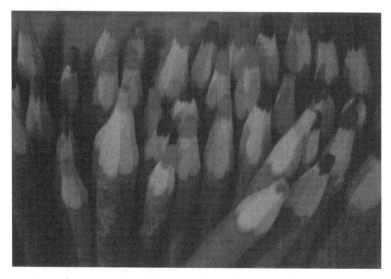

I took a couple pictures of them, and then felt guilty for not buying anything. So I started grabbing some of the crayons that I had in my picture and went to the register. I bought eleven of them and walked out of the store.

And my brother was there. We took them back to his apartment, and I had something to play with while my brother went on with his routines.

The day passed and the night was soon to follow. I got into bed and laid back thinking for awhile. Then I asked through my brother's bedroom door, what the anagram for the colors of the rainbow was. He told me that it was ROY G BIV. With that answer I was able to fall asleep. I woke up in the morning, and after a couple hours, I got into my car and drove home.

I got home and I still didn't feel like I fit in comfortably at home. I was so used to a summer of fitting in everywhere I went. And if I didn't fit in or wasn't comfortable, I just left. I think my year off after college was slowly winding down.

It seemed that what I was fitting into best in the suburbs of Philadelphia was music. I was hanging out with friends and meeting new friends, but I felt best when music was involved.

I went to a local video store that was also a Ticketmaster location, and the people there were pretty nice for the most part. The guy that worked there and I got into a conversation. He told me that if I had never been to Watkins Glen, I should definitely go. And I mentioned that I had never seen the Rolling Stones before, as the posters on the wall said that they were doing their Bridges to Babylon Tour. With a little reluctance, I bought a ticket to the Rolling Stones show in Buffalo and planned to go to Watkins Glen afterward.

I left for Buffalo and I found it. I bought some groceries and went to the parking lot where the concert was. I cooked up what was an original dish for me, all done with my camping stove. I think that it was the best part of the evening.

I woke up the next morning. I took a look at my map and started driving toward Watkins Glen. When I got there, I bought a ticket to hike through the gorge. Afterward, I drove around looking for a nice place. I found a coffee shop–type place called The Professor's Place. I met a girl there, and she said that she would love to stay and talk longer, but her friend Sarah was having some family problems and she was on her way over.

The 5th World

It ended up that when Sarah got there, she and I hit it off. We had a lot in common, so we spent some time together. I had plans to be in New York City with my brother for Yom Kippur, but that didn't work out. I stayed with Sarah for a couple extra days in Watkins Glen.

Eventually, I felt as though I really should be getting to New York City. And I left Sarah and her friends in the Finger Lakes area. Since it was the middle of the week, my brother was really busy. I got to see him for lunch the next day, and back to Philadelphia I went.

I got home and it had been a little over a year since I graduated. There really wasn't any place that I wanted to go to, but I still didn't want to be at home. I talked on the phone with Sarah and considered moving up to New York. I also spent time with Jen, who had become a consistent friend over the years. And if I wanted to hear music, I wouldn't go much farther than Philadelphia.

I was trying to live the lifestyle of being on the road, but without the road. So as my body remained in the same place, my mind would travel wherever and whenever. Being in the same place started to come with stressors and

...and I awoke

pressures that I wasn't ready to address. I no longer had the wide open spaces and country roads that I had grown accustomed to. I also had to deal with the dysfunction of old relationships that I didn't have on the road by myself. There were pressures to live up to the same expectations that I did before I had left for college five years ago, and that wasn't going to happen. But I tried. I tried to be the perfect son, the perfect brother, the hard-working, all-around, can-do guy. And I also tried to be the enlightened soul that I had become. Well the pressure on me became infectious. And that became problematic. So I tried to do what I could do to fix that, but I was up against a losing battle.

My mother felt that she needed help. Help for herself and help for me that she couldn't give me. When she got to her wits' end, she "asked" me to go with her to the Bryn Mawr Hospital Inpatient Psychiatric Unit. I loved and trusted my mother, so I said okay. We got to the hospital, and after a bunch of paperwork, my mother asked me to voluntarily admit myself by signing on the line.

After I signed the paperwork to admit myself, a doctor asked me a few questions. I think that the only one that I said yes to was that sometimes I did have racing thoughts. My mother left and I got a room. Slowly, all the stress and pressure melted away. It almost felt like I was on a vacation.

I ended up making the best of the situation. I played Ping-Pong, watched the movie *Michael*, and watched the Marlins win the World Series. To get my exercise, I would walk laps around the unit with my Walkman. For fresh air, I would go outside during the designated smoking times. During one smoking time, sometime around the third day there, I was standing up, facing Bryn Mawr Avenue. As I stood there staring off at the road, I felt and saw a blue light slowly surrounding me. In a moment, the blue light and I became one and the same. And in that moment I believe that I became the embodiment of Archangel Michael.

The smoke time was over and we went inside. Later that day, my mother, father and step-mother came for a meeting with the doctor about my situation. In the meeting, the doctor said that I was doing well. He recommended certain outpatient steps that I should take. He was ready to discharge me from the hospital, and he asked me if I had anything to say. I said yes. I got that

...and I awoke

same feeling that I had when I was asked to address the group at the spiritual workshop in New Orleans. I felt as though I knew that I wasn't going to get my way, but I still had to speak my peace. This time I was addressing my mother.

My mother had been a believer in the New Age movement when I was only in middle school. She had New Age books and pictures of angels all over the house. I turned to her and asked her if she believed me that I was the embodiment of Archangel Michael. She said no, and we went home.

CHAPTER 11

I graduated college with a bachelor of science degree in psychology. But an undergraduate degree only does so much to prepare someone to deal with a diagnosis personally. I spent the first five months of 1998 trying to understand what it meant to be bipolar. I worked with a therapist once a week on the hard facts. We worked on getting me to accept my diagnosis in my time, and to accept that my reality was not the only reality. I had to learn how to incorporate some of my reality with mainstream reality, and vice versa. And there I could find some relief from the difficult situations that I was dealing with.

To get myself out of the house, I would pick up easy little jobs. I worked part-time delivering catered Italian food. I got to be in my car. I got to listen to my music with a degree of freedom that was nice. At night I would occasionally go to see Splintered Sunlight, the Grateful Dead cover band that played once a week at Brownies.

After about five months of therapy, I felt well enough to go back out into society with the label that I had accepted to wear. I looked through the want ads in the local newspaper and found a summer day camp that was looking for someone to run a two-week soccer camp at the beginning of the summer. I was happily surprised to get hired to run the camp. I was very nervous, but I ran the camp without a hitch. After the two weeks, the owner of the camp asked me to stay on to help out the rest of the summer.

The owner needed someone to help out with canoeing, and be a substitute counselor, and run the softball camp that was coming up later in the summer. And my favorite part of the job was that I became the designated chaperone on all the field trips. It was a lot of fun, and it didn't hurt my self-esteem to feel valued. As the summer was coming to an end, I looked for a similar job, since everything was going so well.

...and I awoke

I got hired to be a teacher's assistant at a Montessori preschool. All this time I was checking in with my therapist, Jodi, every week. Around this time I began to get more involved with living with my diagnosis, since I had begun to accept it. I went to speak with a transpersonal psychologist every other week. At first, I went to speak with him because that was what I wanted to do for my career. When I spoke with him, I almost felt like we were colleagues. Another thing I tried was going to meetings for people with bipolar disorder. I found the meetings rewarding, and that is all that really mattered.

I was enjoying my job at the preschool. Everyone was nice to me, and after a month or so, I fell right into a routine that worked. Once I fell into place, I started opening up to the children. There were well behaved, smart, cute little three-, four- and five-year olds. It was probably Halloween, when I saw all them dressed up in their little Halloween costumes, that I fell in love with them.

A couple months later came Christmastime. One of the five-year-old girls named Marina came up to me and handed me my Christmas present. It was ten free passes

The 5th World

to get into Brownies. She and I went back and forth with excitement, and then her father came over. Her father and Uncle Joe were the owners. So from then on, when I went to Brownies, I felt a little more at home and a little more important because I was teaching the owner's kids.

Once I had become more comfortable and felt that I belonged there more than I did before, my experiences started to blossom. With the added confidence, my ability to connect with people more deeply became possible. Day after day at the preschool and a couple nights a week at either the meetings or at Brownies, or even synagogue I was really starting to open up. I was still seeing Jodi once a week, but I was also seeing people the way I saw people after the experience in New Orleans.

For the past three and a half years since the experience with the car's horn, I knew that I had an ability to see more of a person then just their face. For the first three and a half years, I would see someone, and then it usually took me some time to process in my mind who they were to me. The Tyson-Holyfield fight was probably the first time I saw someone and within the same day I was able to figured

…and I awoke

out what was of importance that I just saw. With the person that I met at the redwood forest, I was able to make a realization in the same day. And I realized part of the significance of Gabriel from Berkeley while in his presence.

In Philadelphia during the beginning of 1999, I was slowly becoming overwhelmed. Everywhere I went there were more and more people of significance. It was either reincarnations of famous people or angels or reincarnations of people that were close family.

I stopped seeing my transpersonal psychologist because he and I had finished our work for the time being, and we both knew it. I kept seeing Jodi, who had been my older sister in a past life in Egypt. I still needed her help. The preschool was filled with so many souls of matter that I will wait for a later part to list some of them. And I will do the same with all the people that I met at Brownies. It was also at this time that looking back at grade school, college, and other people that I had met was very difficult but becoming a little bit more possible with every day that I lived my life openly in the suburbs of Philadelphia.

The 5th World

By the fourth month of 1999, my body began to break down from the workload that I was doing. I got sick in April, just a run-of-the-mill sickness from working with kids. But a week later, I was still sick and I didn't feel like I was going to get any better. I decided that for my own well-being I would not go back to work. I made plans and a week later I got in my car to drive down South. Hopefully, down South I could get some of the relaxation that I needed that I couldn't get in the Northeast.

I drove to Jacksonville, Florida, to see a friend from high school. Then I went over to Sarasota to see the house that my father was going to move into in a few months. I couldn't find his house, but I did find the white sand public beach. I went swimming in the Gulf of Mexico, something that you really can't do from New Orleans. After swimming, I returned to my towel on the beach. I met a young boy with curly hair who was right next to me. Just to play with him, I asked him how old he was, and he replied, "four." I spoke to his mother for a moment, and as he walked away, I realized that I had just met the reincarnation of Jimi Hendrix.

...and I awoke

After spending a few days in Sarasota, I drove south toward Miami. I called my aunt and uncle, and we had dinner just outside of Miami. Later that night, I met up with a fraternity brother and had a drink. We talked for a couple of hours, and then I returned to my hotel.

I woke up in the morning and wasn't very motivated to do anything. Then the idea of going to Jazz Fest in New Orleans came to my mind from something that my fraternity brother had said, and now it seemed possible. I started the drive from Miami to New Orleans. A little more than twelve hours later, New Orleans was in my sights but I couldn't stay awake. I was about forty five miles from Jazz Fest, and I was on fumes.

I pulled into a truck stop and walked around as I got two ice cold sodas. As I was in line to pay for the sodas, I started looking around at the tapes that they had for sale. I thought that maybe some new music would get me through the last hour. I picked up Jewel's *Spirit* album.

I got in my car and started to drive again. I put on *Spirit* by Jewel. I had a soda in one hand and the steering wheel in the other. All of the sudden, I began to respond very well to the new music and soda. I felt like I was flying again, and getting to New Orleans was a breeze.

I parked my car in Jesus' parking lot, got my ticket, and went inside. I heard Walter "Wolfman" Washington playing his guitar. It drew me to him, and once I found a nice grassy place, my body just collapsed into the music and all the people at the festival.

Later that night, I saw The Funky Meters play a show. At the show I saw a bunch of my fraternity brothers, including my old roommate Matt and his girlfriend. After the show was over, they were all heading downtown to their hotel rooms. But I wanted to go back to the neighborhood that we all lived in near the university. I went to a bar on Oak Street, just next to where I lived. I stayed there until the morning and then got some sleep at a friend's house.

The next morning I woke and got into my car. I started driving north. I got to Philadelphia, Mississippi, and got off the highway. I got a hotel room and a proper night of rest.

The next day I made it to Tennessee and drove around aimlessly for a while. After lunch, I met a couple of guys that ran a go-cart track, so that was what I did with my afternoon. It started to get a little dark, and one of the guys at the go-cart track told me of a nice little motel down the road. I got a room, and the first thing that I did was go swimming in the Ocoee River. The rest of the night I kept trying to write the way it sounded in my head and the way it felt in my heart. After a little while, I must have made a breakthrough, because what I was writing had rhythm and information. It was that night that I found my voice as a writer.

CHAPTER 12

I felt accomplished. Accomplished enough to go and see my younger brother at the end of his senior year of college. I got to College Park, Maryland, and spent a couple days at my brother's apartment. He introduced me to his friends and his girlfriend and her father, who happened to be in town the same time that I was. After the few days, I didn't want to overstay my welcome, and I headed north to Philadelphia.

When I got back to Philadelphia in early May, I was feeling good again. Relaxed and reenergized. I would wake up when I naturally woke up. Slowly get out of bed. Usually, I would make my way down the street to the neighborhood park. When I got tired of hearing the same sounds from the people and the cars, I pulled out my Walkman and a tape and was back in heaven.

One day I was driving by the park, and I noticed a softball team practicing. I was always up to play if the people were up to having me. I walked up and made some small talk with the ladies on the bench. I pointed out that they didn't have a short fielder, so one of the ladies said if I wanted to play, to ask. I asked the softball team if they wanted a short fielder, and they said sure. By the end of the practice, I was on the team.

I started feeling like I was wasting some of my time, so I went looking for a job. In the next part of the book, I go into much further detail about the job that I got and everything else that went with it. In this part of the book, I will pick up with my mother and her business partner picking me up at Delaware County Correctional about two weeks later. I had gone off of my medication for the first time in the year and half that I had been taking it. I went off of it when I left for Florida.

My mother agreed on my behalf to take me to the hospital in Norristown early the next day, to get me back on

...and I awoke

my medications. After being picked up from jail, we went home. I had one night of good food and rest. The next morning I was off to spend the Memorial Day weekend in another mental hospital.

Once I got to the hospital, the reincarnation experiences started up at full force. The intensity and quantity of the experiences were similar to when I had left Philadelphia to go down South to get a break from it. Well, my break was over. By the end of the weekend, I had spent time with the present incarnations of Michelangelo, Leonardo da Vinci, Socrates, Vivaldi, the person who was Nostradamus and the apostle Mark, and a woman named Susan who was Raphael the Renaissance artist and is the archangel Raphael.

When I got out of the hospital, I picked up where I had left off. I went out to The Point in Bryn Mawr because it seemed like a great place to go and just be myself. I went there on an open mic night to meet someone there. The girl that I planned to meet there wasn't there, but I met a girl named Joanna there that night. She and I became instant friends. The two of us spent a lot of time together over the next couple months.

Besides hanging out with Joanna, I spent a lot of time with a friend named Jason, who I met at one of the meetings for people with bipolar disorder. I also spent a lot of my time at the park meeting what seemed to be a famous soul a day. And I finished the season with the softball team.

I had the honor of playing softball with our third basemen who was the apostle Philip in a past life. The coach, catcher, and backup pitcher's name was Scott, and he was Babe Ruth in one past life and my grandson in his lifetime before that. And after one game at the JCC, the regular pitcher had a girlfriend who took the three of us and her son, who was close to two, out to Dairy Queen. I hung out with the three of them for a little while, and about a week later, I consciously realized that the young boy was the incarnation of the soul of Kurt Cobain and my grandson from my lifetime before the one I shared with the coach.

Toward the end of the summer, I was at Joanna's place of work. I walked outside, and I saw Jessica sitting there. I had to approach her, because ignoring her was not an option. I said hi, and she repeated the pleasantry. There was an uncomfortable moment, so I started to walk away,

...and I awoke

and she stopped me to tell me that she had gone back to school for some postgraduate classes. It was nice to know that we were okay.

When the summer was over, I signed up at the JCC, Jewish Community Center. Around this time I also enjoyed the party mentality that was going on for the end of the millennium and the beginning of the new one.

Around March of 2000, a couple months after my grandmother passed away, I decided that I was going to move to Flagstaff, Arizona, to write my book. I told myself that I would leave a year from then, which gave me plenty of time to finish up my business in Philadelphia. After this decision, I went out to get another job to make the most of my time there. I got another job delivering food for Bryn Mawr Pizza. Then the summer of 2000 came, and I got a job working with children with autism. After meeting everyone that worked there and getting to know the children that were signed up for the camp, I was sadly informed by my boss that we weren't there to try and help them get better but just to watch over them. It was summer camp, not a school. There was one child in particular that I was moved to help. But the boss gave me an ultimatum: to either let the kids play or, if I couldn't do that, I would have to leave. My hands were tied, so I left.

I spent the next couple weeks talking about how excited I was to move to Arizona. By October, everyone, including my mother, had heard enough about it and told me that it was time for me to go. I packed up the U-Haul and started to drive. Before I drove out of Philadelphia, and after I left my crying mother, I stopped at the park. I wanted to say good-bye to three friends that I had made over the years. I thought that it would be fun to act as though I was like one of them now with my U-Haul truck. They were UPS drivers, and they drove around in their trucks. When I got into the U-Haul I thought that maybe that was what it felt like to drive one of those big trucks.

As I drove around the corner to the park, they were getting in their trucks and starting to go back to work. With a bit of pride, I stopped and talked to the third for a moment. So the Four Horsemen rode off, each in their own direction. Mine was southwest, to write my book.

PART II

9 / 10

9 / 10

I opened the door of my forty-dollar motel room and had a moment in the California desert. The stagnant heat had the feeling of three in the afternoon in Flagstaff, and it was somewhere around 9:30 a.m. in Joshua Tree.

I started looking around for my literary agent. She had converted one of the motel rooms into her office. We had an appointment around ten or eleven o'clock, when she was going to type up a contract for her to officially become the literary agent for my first book.

At some time around ten or eleven o'clock, she opened her office and sat down at her typewriter to personalize the contract. That was my first clue that I wasn't getting what I wanted, a business person who still used an old-fashioned typewriter in the year 2001. Being a person of faith, I let it slide with hopes that she would still be able to do her job efficiently. After the contract was typed up, we both signed it, and I paid my fee.

I felt quite badly about the entire trip to Joshua Tree, but I believed in my diligent work ethic to succeed. The excitement I felt that my book was going to get published and that I was going to begin a new life of fame and fortune were my overwhelming feelings. These feelings of elation began to outweigh my feeling of sadness that I experienced in Joshua Tree as I drove along the snake highway on the way out of California and back into Arizona.

If you have driven on any of those roads, you may know why I called it a snake highway. The road is one lane each way, with a speed limit around 50 or 60 mph. This road was in a desolate area, and it was made to ensure that you don't go too quickly. Imagine speed bumps on a 60 mph road, but instead of a speed bump that is one or two feet long, these bumps were about seventy feet long and about eight feet high. The road serpentined vertically like a roller coaster: nauseating, unique and kind of fun.

As I was finishing the adventure of driving this road, I was leaving behind my Joshua Tree experience and driving excitedly back to Flagstaff. All I wanted to do was share my happiness and excitement with my friends. I now know how it worked out with that version of my book, but I couldn't ignore the positivity that my friends were showing me, and I won't belittle how much I learned from the experience.

As soon as I got home, I went over to Jacque's for a celebration drink. I was greeted and welcomed when I got there. I allowed myself to have the fun that I felt I deserved. My friends came by to spend their evening at the bar, and I was happy to include them in my celebration. Afternoon turned into evening, and evening turned into night, and before I wanted it to be, it was closing time.

I do remember one moment before the evening turned into a big night of big emotions. Scott stopped me as I was going on and on in celebration and asked me to pinky swear to him that I was telling the truth that this was the end of the book. I did swear that I was done that book, but neither he nor I knew that there was going to be a second, bigger and better version later down the road.

To me, Scott was one of the most significant people that ever stepped foot in that bar. He was my first child, my oldest son, and the father of Scott my softball coach in my second lifetime, twenty thousand years ago in Atlantis. He was also Andrew Mellon in another past life, one of the many famous businessmen that spent time in that bar.

Maybe business theory isn't my specialty. I can't say that there is a business theory out there that I know of that I agree with. I think that that is so because the business world, unlike religion, philosophy, and medicine but like the legal world, has not fully accepted socialism as the foundation of all functional systems. Not the socialism of Marx and Engle, which always ends in a fight, but the socialism of the twelve tribes of Israel, the one that works out peacefully. I feel like the business world and the legal world are so wrapped up in perversions of money, power, truth, and reality that they have forgotten that it is all about people primarily, and the money and power will come.

So the night went until 2:00 a.m., and home I went. At around nine o'clock in the morning, I was jolted out of a deep slumber and seemingly automatically made my way into the living room and turned on the TV. I saw a picture of one of the towers of the World Trade Center with smoke coming out from near the top. I thought I was watching a movie or something created in Hollywood. Then I started listening to the panicked voices, and quickly I started to wake up. And before I could completely get a grasp of what I was seeing on the TV, there was another plane flying into the second tower. I couldn't believe what I was seeing.

I was twenty-five hundred miles away from where all of this was going on. But I felt the chaos and the panic as if I were there. Still very anxious, I felt completely safe as I was watched it from a distance on TV.

The next thing I remember is going over to Jacque's around twelve o'clock, just to be around other people, hoping to at least make some sense of what I just saw and what I was feeling. Jacque wasn't there, but I knew that she wouldn't be. I knew that it was Nina's shift. Nina was the day bartender: a strong woman with a soft side. I knew she was able to talk about things of matter with an empathetic touch, and that is why I headed over to Jacque's.

She grew up farther away from New York than Flagstaff, so it seemed as though she wasn't as connected to what was going on, but definitely as concerned. We tried to make as much sense of the events as possible. I had gotten to Jacque's after the plane crashed into the Pentagon, which was about one mile from where my younger brother was living. I also arrived after the plane had landed in western Pennsylvania, which seemed to be on its way to come and get me out in Arizona. My younger brother has since informed me that the plane had actually done a U-turn and was planning another attack on Washington DC.

Nina and I watched the TV with concern as I told her that my older brother lives in Manhattan but was living in London for work at the time. So on one level, I was feeling that two planes crashed where my older brother lived and one crashed where my younger brother lived; and the last plane was, on some level, coming for me in Arizona and was brought down in the state that all three of us were born in, Pennsylvania. I truly do believe that there is some coincidence, but the reality is way too far out of reach.

Then Nina and I sat back and watched the city of New York go through horrors that most people can't even imagine. I still can't believe what I saw and felt for those people that jumped from the first tower's stories above where the plane crashed into it. And I felt for all those people that were on the streets with nowhere to go, except to just keeping going.

Then the TV showed a man videotaping the white-gray cloud that was created by the falling of one or both of the towers. He said to the camera that it was as though day had turned into night, and those words stuck with me. Those words that the man in Manhattan spoke still continue to ring true when I think about that signs of the apocalypse. The fifth sign of the apocalypse is that "day will turn into night," as it did.

I got involved in the signs of the apocalypse at the end of the summer of 1999. At that time I was spending my afternoons in the beautiful, sunny weather of the suburbs of Philadelphia. Around eleven or twelve o'clock in the afternoon, I would make my way down to the park, where I would walk around the park, listening to whatever Grateful

Dead or other musician's tape caught my interest. This was before the iPod; at the time I was driving a '92 automobile that still had a tape player in the radio, not a fancy CD player. I could have upgraded my music collection to CDs, but I still had endearing emotions toward tapes, probably at least because of the Grateful Dead.

At around eleven or twelve, I would be walking around the park, and it seemed that most days that summer were beautiful sunny days. Eventually I would make it to the upper half of the park, where there was more wide open space. I would make my way over to a set or two of bleachers near the street, under a bunch of trees, and there I would talk to three guys that worked for UPS that were on their lunch break.

We would normally have small talk: about their day and how much of their work they were getting done, or about sports or family. But one day, after getting to know them for weeks, I opened up a conversation with a religious question, "What do you guys know about the signs of the apocalypse?" This question came out of the clear blue sky. But surprisingly, after a moment or two of joke cracking, they saw that I was still there and still interested. So we started talking about it. We focused on the Four Horsemen of the apocalypse.

I remember a conversation that we had on the topic of the Four Horsemen of the apocalypse took place on a Friday. I remember that as the conversation was coming together, there was a flock of small black birds that flew over us in a chaotic formation that reminded me of the dancing and the music that I had heard the night before.

So I stood on the upper field of the neighborhood park, by the bleachers that are near the street, and I had this conversation with three men that drove their big, brown UPS trucks. We playfully started to see if we could figure out which one of us would be which horseman. We took into consideration that the signs of the apocalypse were to be considered prophecy, and prophecy is considered a form of art.

So we would have to treat the identification of the Four Horsemen as though it was a piece of art. We were evolving a creation of art, by interpreting what was already there and shedding new light on it by furthering the creation. We were not recreating anything but evolving something that was already in existence, because what we were doing was brand new and enriched the previous artwork. We decided who Slaughter was, who Famine was, and who Death was, and that I would be Conquest, because I guess that that was what I did. I was becoming known for the side of my personality that was becoming an efficient and effective, peaceful warrior.

My experience with the fourth sign of the apocalypse started some time in the summer of 1999. The fifth sign, "day turning into night," occurred in 2001.

The sixth sign of the apocalypse occurred in late 2004 in the Indian Ocean. In December of 2004, the earth opened up and swallowed a lot of water, then spit it back up. From this natural act, a tsunami was created, killing many people. One person that did survive the tsunami was the 2003 *Sports Illustrated* swimsuit cover girl, Petra Nemcova.

She was in Thailand with her fiancé, who did not survive the tsunami, when it hit ground. Petra spent eight hours holding onto a palm tree until it was safe enough to leave. She spent three weeks in a Thai hospital recovering from numerous broken bones and internal injuries. Through everything that this lady endured, she still stands strongly and encourages those affected by the Tsunami to have a happy heart.

In the time that I have been writing this part of my book, Osama Bin Laden has been killed under the orders of President Obama. The death of Bin Laden has brought some closure for many people, including myself. With the closure of Bin Laden's life, a door has been opened, at least for me, to explain all seven signs of the apocalypse with greater elaboration.

Let's start with the first sign of the apocalypse. Life was well during the early '90s. People were happy, the hippies and yuppies (West Coast and East Coast) were coming together, and life was good.

Then came David Koresh, the embodiment of the first sign of the apocalypse: the false prophet. The first sign of the apocalypse is that there will be the coming of a false prophet. David Koresh was that false prophet. And in February of 1993, with the help from the US Bureau of

Alcohol, Tobacco and Firearms, the first seal of the apocalypse was torn open.

From here we will move onto the second sign. The second sign of the apocalypse is the coming of the false teacher. In January 1998, the seal to the second sign of the apocalypse was broken when America's number one teacher looked straight into the camera and said that he "did not have sexual relations with that woman."

Bill Clinton broke the second seal with that infamous line. He opened the door for false teachers to enter this world and do as they pleased. Soon teaching perversions of the truth became the norm, shown ad nauseam by the next president of the United States.

Now as we get into the third and fourth signs, I must say a few words. I am writing this story because I am actually the only person that can. The first two signs (along with the last three) are common knowledge events. The third sign is not common knowledge and is only recognized by a handful of people. Then there is the fourth sign, which occurred in relatively the same place (five miles away from each other) in the suburbs of Philadelphia. The fourth sign has an even smaller handful of people involved. And from the handful of people involved in the third sign and the handful of people involved in the fourth sign, I am the only person with firsthand knowledge of both events.

The third sign of the apocalypse is the coming of false authority. I had returned from a vacation during the beginning of May 1999. I had visited Florida, Jazz Fest in New Orleans, and a small river town in Tennessee where I found the voice to my writing style. I returned to Philadelphia after spending a couple days in College Park, Maryland, with my younger brother as he was getting ready to graduate.

I got back to Philly and decided to get a job. I found a chicken restaurant on Villanova University's campus that was looking for a delivery guy. I have always liked to keep moving, so delivery jobs are usually what I found. I walked in and was hired on the spot and was asked to work the next day.

I became friendly with the girl that took orders at the register. She was almost eighteen, and I was twenty-five. We had fun playing around, wasting time with each other.

The 5th World

After being back in Philly for about a week, I started looking for new and exciting things to do. Karen, the girl who ran the register, came up with the idea for the two of us to work out together at her gym. She said that she was a member and she could get a guest in for free. We made plans to go the next day at noon since neither of us were working.

I showed up at her house at noon as planned, and she was on the phone screaming at someone, and she informed me that she hadn't done her chores yet. So I told her that I would come back in an hour, and she carelessly agreed.

I returned in an hour or two, and it was as though I had never left. She was still on the phone screaming, and she hadn't even started her chores. But now she was screaming at me about her mother coming home. I was getting a little too old for this kind of behavior, and I felt as though it was my time to leave.

As I was leaving, this little ten-year-old boy was walking pretty much right to where I was standing by my car in the middle of the street. I asked him if he knew Karen. He said, "Of course. She is my sister." He invited me to come back up the driveway, and I said sure with the hope that things might still work out.

I asked if he wanted to play basketball, he said no and asked if I wanted to climb the tree in his backyard. I hesitated for a moment when I remembered my age, but I gave it a try anyway. We both climbed the tree and sat on the fence, and then he went inside. Karen was still on the phone screaming with somebody, so I screamed good-bye and left.

I went home and just wanted to decompress. That girl was high stress when she wasn't at work. After a couple hours of relaxing, I decided to go for a walk. I stepped out of my house and down my driveway, and as I crossed the street, I saw a police van down on the corner. This was very strange for my neighborhood, but it didn't stop me. I still wanted to go for a walk and burn off some of the residual stress.

I walked through the neighborhood on the way to the park, and then I saw another police car drive in front of me at the crossroad. What might have been ten seconds later,

I heard someone say "Michael" in my ear. I turned to look, and it was the police officer that was parked on the corner (which was about five minutes earlier).

The officer asked if he could talk with me, and I knew I was in trouble, but I had no idea what I had done wrong. A couple of Lower Merion police officers, including the one that had addressed me, asked me to wait there because the police from Havertown wanted to talk to me.

The Havertown police arrived and told me that I knew what this was about, but I didn't. Although, it was clear that Havertown police wanted to talk to me, and I was just in Havertown about two hours ago. So they asked if I would come down to their station so they could talk to me. Eventually I agreed to go with them, and off to the Havertown Police Station we went.

I got in the police car and was driven down Darby Road to the police station. There were two police officers that were grilling me about what I did wrong. I had no idea what they were talking about. They were making comments as though I had done something immoral with this seventeen-year-old girl, her ten-year-old brother, and their property. After about a half hour of this Havertown police officer trying to get me to admit to doing something that I didn't do, a third officer came into the small room. After a few intense minutes, the first police officer stood up and declared that I was under arrest. And that was the third sign of the apocalypse, the coming of false authority.

The fourth sign of the apocalypse was broken later as I left Philadelphia for Flagstaff in the fall of 2000. The fifth sign occurred on 9/11/01, and the sixth was the Indian tsunami, "when the earth would open up and swallow itself."

The seventh and last sign was Hurricane Katrina, "when the roads would flow with blood." The seventh sign, Hurricane Katrina, actually occurred ten years after I had my vision on the corner of Broadway and St. Charles in New Orleans: late August/early September 1995 and late August/early September 2005.

Before you take a breath and exhale, the next part will begin. When the seventh sign of the apocalypse had been completed, the next phase had begun: The Seven Year War.

The Seven Year War is the war between the fallen angels and the three Antichrists versus God. Some people refer to the Seven Year War as the war between God and Satan; this is not incorrect, but it is very general. A more detailed explanation would be that the Seven Year War is a war in which God must defeat Mephistopheles (the angel of worry), Satan (the angel of fear), Beelzebub (the angel of pain), the Devil (the angel of hate), and Lucifer (the angel of death).

Once God had systematically defeated each of the five fallen angels, then God faced off against each of the three Antichrists. Once the three Antichrists were defeated, the Seven Year War came to an end. Many people, including myself see the end of the Seven Year War to have been on December 21, 2012. This day was the end of the old world and the beginning of the new one, the 5th World.

PART III

THE MATERIAL WORLD OF ANGELS

THE MATERIAL WORLD OF ANGELS

After years of experiences, I have come to find an existence that can only be defined as The Material World of Angels. The knowledge about The Material World of Angels is from the perspective that I received in New Orleans, after the sound of the car's horn pierced my soul. And along with my perspective, comes a purpose for the knowledge. The existence of The Material World of Angels as I see it is a way of identification and therapy. This way of identification and therapy's purpose focuses on balancing and developing the mental, emotional, and physical aspects of the being.

In any school or class, it takes work and devotion to achieve your desired goal. This way of identification and therapy is like any other: diligence and commitment are necessary for success. The identification begins with the acceptance of your experiences. By remembering and staying with your experiences, you are able to live with and be with any thought, feeling, or sensation that may arise.

The therapy starts when any conflicting aspect of your life is settled correctly. Once settled, there is a sense of neutrality: when the solution balances the conflict. Once balanced and having a neutral charge, the neutralized stimulus begins its accent through The Material World of Angels. The Material World of Angels is a therapeutic lifestyle that becomes second nature, if performed correctly time and time again.

I will now start listing the different kinds of angels and their purposes, giving brief explanations of each level of the angels within The Material World of Angels. Within these brief explanations, I hope that the reader will find a similarity to one of the angelic levels that he or she feels resembles them. If you are correct in identifying the level that feels right to you, you very well may have found your angelic identity. I say this because it is my belief that all people are angels, of one kind or another. I will give a little information that I hope will assist you in finding yourself within The Material World of Angels.

I think it is important for the reader to know that there are approximately five hundred Angels at the bottom level, and I am finding more every year. There are only seven Archangels at the second level. Of the five hundred or so Angels on the first level, I know just about all of them. And as for the seven Archangels, I surely know all seven of them. That leaves the five higher levels of angels and if the reader was to find themselves in The Material World of Angels it would most likely be in one of the higher five levels. It is important to say that there may be hundreds of millions of angels that create each of the five higher levels of The Material World of Angels. As for the five hundred Angels and seven Archangels, I haven't met all of them face to face in a traditional sense. I have either met them or have seen them on television or listened to them through some form of media.

It is important to realize that this way of therapy has a linear structure, so that one step leads to the next. It is also important to realize that getting to the top level is not the goal of this way of therapy. The goal is becoming a balanced and developed person in The Material World of Angels. I feel that the lowest level of angel "matters" the most since those angels are closest to accepted, mainstream life on earth. The highest level is least obvious, and therefore most difficult to recognize or to be conscious of their existence.

LEVEL 1: ANGELS

I will start with the lowest building block and those that are closest to existence on Earth. The lowest block in this way of therapy's structure is the block called Angels.

The lowest block consists of hundreds of dualities, or opposites, that are meant to provoke a response from each other until the charged response is neutralized by its opposite. For an example of something that provokes a response is the emotion of hate. If an Angel or person doesn't love someone enough, then a negative response will be created. Chaos, or feeling Uncomfortable, may be the created response. Then Order will search out the Chaos, and Comfort will be attracted to the feeling of Uncomfortable because of its desire to feel Comfortable.

This is the logical, functional purpose of the Angels. Once the Angel of Comfort has neutralized the Angel of Uncomfortable, then the Angel of Order works on neutralizing the response by the Angel of Chaos. Once neutralized, the Angel of Hate's response can and will only be balanced and neutralized by the Angel of Love. The opposite of hate is love, and love is the only emotional response that will neutralize the provocative aspect of the emotion of hate in The Material World of Angels. This level of the Angels searches out the opposite Angel with the desire of being accepted and therefore able to be neutralized.

These Angels are gifted with purity of their essence; what they essentially are: Love, Order or Comfort. Like the other levels, at this level of this way of therapy, the Angels have one singular purpose and that is what they do. I feel that an understanding of this level of The Material World of Angels is critical to the functional therapeutic structure of the Angelic World. I say this because the bottom level is by nature the most substantial of the seven levels. To build anything in life that will work, it needs a good, strong foundation.

The Material World of Angels

You can imagine the Angelic World as the process that water goes through in evaporation. When water evaporates, the closer the water molecules are to the ground, the bigger and more substantial they are. As they get into the higher levels of the atmosphere, the water molecules are smaller and less substantial matter. Then they all collect together to create clouds, and that is how I see The Material World of Angels. When the Angelic World has accomplished a goal, it is as if the planet is covered by a white canopy of clouds. When it is time for the Angelic World to take a break, the clouds disappear. And when it is time for The Material World of Angels to work again, the clouds come back together and the matter falls to the earth. The Material World of Angels goes to work making sure not to leave too much substance on the ground, but also not to starve the earth of what it needs to grow. Using moisture as an example, we can see how Angels want to leave a mark where they have been: to help those who need and to replenish and take care of what is already there of themselves.

LEVEL 2: ARCHANGELS

The next level up in The Material World of Angels is the world of the Archangels. The Archangels are considered by me to be the glue that holds the structure together. In this realm there are seven Archangels that are represented by the seven colors of the rainbow and the seven gifts that they share with the Angelic World.

The lowest Archangel of the group of seven is the Archangel of the color Violet. The Archangel of Violet is gifted with Reality. The Archangel of Violet is sort of the gatekeeper to the next level of angels. The dualities, or Angels, are not given clearance into the next level unless they have neutralized themselves. Once the Archangel of Reality has given the neutralized Angel the okay to pass through the door, then the accepted and neutralized stimulus is considered Real, in The Material World of Angels.

While in the color of The Archangel of Violet, the stimulus learns what is Real. It is here that the Archangel explains the difference of reality on Earth and Reality in the Angelic World. For example, the neutralized stimulus of fear and not afraid may enter the level of the Archangel of Violet's world. The stimulus experience a new existence without duality: a world of one Reality that is simple and true. That stimulus, or joining of two souls, is able to experience Reality made up entirely of their work. If they worked functionally and diligently and continue to work that way, their Reality becomes a better and better experience.

The next Archangel is the Archangel of Indigo. This Archangel has the gift of Expression. The Archangel of Indigo takes the ever-growing Reality and finds verbal and nonverbal ways of Expressing Reality: Expressions of Reality in its purest sense. Some say that music is the way the angels express themselves to humans, others say artwork is the true form; some think sex is their purest Expression. Others still say that playing sports or just playing around is the truest Expression, and some believe in the art of conversation. Whichever way you choose, one thing that we all can agree on is that the Archangel of Indigo is the Archangel of Expression.

The third level is the color of Blue. The Archangel of Blue's gift is Connectivity: the one who brings the clouds together. Like all the raindrops come together to create a cloud, the Archangel of Blue, or as Archangel Michael, I keep all the Expressions of Reality interconnected.

The next level is the Archangel of the color Green, gifted with Timing. This Archangel takes the collection of Expressions of Reality and creates a flow that is perfectly timed. Another word for this is synchronicity.

The level of the Archangel of Yellow has the gift of Transcendence. The Archangel of Yellow, or Archangel Raphael, takes the Realistic Expressions that are held together and work in synchronicity to another level.

The next level is the level of the Archangel of Orange. The gift, or attribute of the Archangel of Orange is Perspective. Once the Expressions of Reality have been held interconnected and are working in synchronicity, the

Archangel Raphael moves the stimulus to another level. Once on this transcendent level, the Archangel of Orange takes an angelic look at what there is to be seen and realizes, with mind, heart, body, and soul a Perspective that is the one true Perspective in The Material World of Angels.

The last and highest Archangel is the Archangel of the color Red. The Archangel of Red, or Archangel Gabriel, is gifted with Passion. First, Archangel Gabriel receives the Expressions of Reality that are held together and work with angelic Timing at a Transcendent level. Then that which has Transcended is Perceived with conscious awareness, and Archangel Gabriel gives passion, or life, to the Perceptions.

I do believe that it was the Passion of Archangel Gabriel that pierced my soul on that day in New Orleans: the sound of a horn that opened my eyes in the mystical sense.

LEVEL 3: CHERUBS

After making your way through the understanding of the beginning level of Angels and taking the seven arduous steps of the Archangels, the person experiencing The Material World of Angels is given a bit of an intellectual reprieve, maybe. The level of Angels is mentally demanding because of the constant work with dualities. The level of the seven Archangels is mentally demanding because of the amount of attention and importance that the Archangels stand for. The next step, or third level, is the level of the Cherubs, and though you still have to work to understand them, the reward is very pleasurable.

The Cherubs can be experienced by those who live for fun. Witty, highbrow humor whose reward is a feeling of laughing, as though nothing else exists and the laughter will go on forever. At the level of the Cherubs in The Material World of Angels, the doctor says that laughter is the best medicine.

LEVEL 4: MANNERS

The fourth level of angels are called the Manners. They are called the Manners because their way is always to be an example of good and correct behavior. These angels are naturally on their best behavior all of the time. When the Manners create patterns of good behavior, they are sometimes referred to as rules of etiquette or manners. Some say that it is the Manners that make the civilized world of The Material World of Angels go round.

LEVEL 5: VALUES

The fifth level of angels is the Values. Angels are constantly going back and forth with duality, Archangels are rarely ever satisfied with their work, Cherubs are great, but they are always looking for a happy medium, the Manners are wonderful but so truly unappreciated in the world today. Then there are the Values. They have one purpose and one purpose only and that is keep their attention on the person, animal, plant, or thing that is most important at the time.

I have deeply studied the Values out of necessity. Because when you have interests like one's meaning in life, or one's purpose on this planet, or the importance of figuring out what really matters to you it is important to keep a healthy perspective. My purpose in The Material World of Angels is to hold everything together, but if it weren't for the Values, I would have never known what to hold on to and what to let go of.

LEVEL 6: PRINCIPLES

It is the Manners that create the habits of good behavior, or manners. Then it is the Values that decide what is truly of importance. Then it is the Principles that stand unwavering for the Manner that focuses on that which is of greatest Value. From the Principles we get healthy characteristics of life like honor and justice in our daily lives.

LEVEL 7: SERAPHIM

The top level of the Angelic World is the Seraphim. The role of the Seraphim is to be an authority looking over those levels below them. When pressure becomes too much at this level, the Seraphim open up and rain on all the other levels, letting the other levels feel what it feels like to be a Seraphim. The Seraphim are meant to be examples of the alpha male or female-the ideal man or woman.

The goal of this way of therapy is to find yourself within the levels and to become the angel that you are. As an angel you can live in a world made up of good habits and constantly try to make bad habits better. In the work to try and better the bad habits, there seems to always be work for someone. It is that work that heals the soul, the mind, the emotions, and the body in The Material World of Angels. .

PART IV

WORLDS ONE THROUGH TWELVE

WORLDS ONE THROUGH TWELVE

After having my experience of awakening, I have tried to do my best with all the information and fulfilling the expectations of satisfactorily communicating said information. I have learned that I will never know as much at once as I did in that moment of awakening for the rest of this lifetime. And because of that I have had to let go of some knowledge and some emotions. But what I have held on to in terms of knowledge and emotion is still quite vast. When I was living in California from late 2002 to early 2006, I was inspired by a system, or structure, to organize my knowledge and emotions. This structure is not only genius, in my opinion, but also very gratifying.

I have created this system, or structure, that reaches deep into the past and far into the future and is able to function in the present.

This structure consists of twelve individual worlds, each of great importance. It starts with the First World, which is the oldest civilized world. For this structure, all time before the beginning of the First World is irrelevant, but the knowledge and emotions from that irrelevant time may someday become relevant, so it is considered to exist. The experiences before the beginning of the First World exist, but are immaterial. The structure ends with the Twelfth World. And likewise, all time after the Twelfth World is meaningless, but as the world evolves, it may become very meaningful. In both cases, if anything is to become something, it would be through the process of the spiritual world becoming part of the material world.

The structure called Worlds One through Twelve is a metaphysical creation with the goal of having each individual world work with each other world. As the worlds systematically cooperate with each other toward its functional goal, then the true goal is realized. The true goal is having Worlds One through Twelve as one unified entity, for the purpose of peaceful and pleasurable existence.

WORLD 1

Before I discuss the First World, I would like to share the aspect of this part of the book that I consider genius. To be able to live in any one of the Twelve Worlds, you are going to need some form of assistance, and that assistance comes in the way of a simple mathematical theory. It takes no more than division and multiplication, but it creates a structure that is priceless.

To give you the first example of it, I will use the First World. The First World began with the birth of the first human being, approximately seventy thousand years ago. This birth took place somewhere in eastern Africa; I believe in Kenya. It was a time of simplicity. It was a time of deep, rich love.

Parts of that world still exist in our everyday moments, and I will begin to prove it. As I was told on the reservation by Emery, the medicine man, we are moving into a new world. They called it world number four, but they never knew of the First World. So for me, I do agree that we are evolving into a new world, but I believe that it is the Fifth World that we are evolving into. And this new world was fully brought into global existence on December 21, 2012.

Being rooted in the Fifth World, and going into the First World, I am going to show you how much each world affects our daily lives in the present. I will do so by using division and separating each world by your inner world and your outer world. To explain the difference between one's inner and outer worlds is quite simple: your skin is what divides the inner world from the outer world.

The world that we are living in is the Fifth World, so that is the constant. The amount of the First World that is still a part of your internal workings is 1/5, the First World divided by the Fifth World, or 20%. The amount of First World that is still outwardly assisting us to make choices in everyday life is 5/1, the Fifth World divided by the First World, or 500%. That means that every time you make a decision, there are four other choices out there that you could choose with 100% certainty. It doesn't mean that all five one hundred percent choices are good, right, or true. It just means that someone experiencing the outer world of the First World has five complete choices to choose from. Sometime that makes for a lot of bad choices before you learn which of the five is the best choice.

Throughout this part of the book, you will receive a brief explanation of each world, to see if you can relate to it or if you can use it as a guide to educate yourself on your existence in the world. After the explanation, I will show the mathematics of how much of each world is affecting us today in the Fifth World.

The primary goal of this part is help people better understand the moment that they are living in, though the primary goal is not the only goal. For me personally, the goal is to study each and every world to the best of my ability. It's also to enjoy the wisdom and gifts of each world and to smooth the rough edges that worlds may have with each other to the best of my ability. This metaphysical creation, which would go under the title of ontology, creates a space that gives life a more genuine perspective.

WORLD 2

World Two is a complicated world. It started some twenty thousand years ago in the area of Tuscany, Italy. At the beginning of the Second World in Italy, or legendary Atlantis, there was a shift. There wasn't as much of a feminine energy as there had been in the First World in Africa, so the energy became more masculine. The balance to this masculine culture was the culture of the Lemurians. The Lemurians lived on the other side of the planet in Peru. My explanation of the beginning of the Second World will be coming from a perspective that is generally Atlantian.

The Atlantians, from half a planet away, were on some level aware of the existence of another culture. Twenty thousand years ago, there were no boats, phones, or other forms of communication that were effective farther than the sound of someone's voice or the distance they would go to give a message. This was unsatisfactory for the masculine, sensitive Atlantians. So a higher level of usage of the human brain was opened. Atlantian minds were soon able to communicate at great distances with only thoughts: telepathy. After telepathy, to satisfy some Atlantian's souls, there was clairvoyance for those who needed to see what was on their minds. I do believe that the Lemurians were gifted with the ability to communicate with emotions beyond the ability of the average human.

The Lemurians began in eastern Africa seventy thousand years ago, just like every other culture. They traveled north and kept on traveling, through Asia and across the Bering Strait.

I believe that the Lemurians as a collective people, or culture, went all the way down to Peru. I also believe that along the travel from Africa to South America, many people stopped and called the place that they stopped home. I believe that a couple popular places to stop were in Alaska, the Pacific Northwest and around southern California, not to mention Mexico, Central America, and other South American civilizations. I believe these cultures do date as far back as possibly just less than twenty thousand years ago. That means that there were Native Americans some twenty thousand years ago along the Pacific Ocean. In time those people moved east. I believe that there were people living in the Southwest some eight thousand years ago. I believe that there were people living on the west side of the Mississippi River around five thousand years ago. And I believe that there were people living on the east side of the Mississippi River thirty five hundred years ago in the South to two thousand years ago in the Northeast.

Obviously, these people are called Native Americans. But it is important to remember that the Hopis consider themselves to be the oldest continual culture in the United States. I know that this information may be confusing, but don't worry about it, I will explain it more in the last part of the book.

The masculine energy of the Atlantians was in a quest for its counterpart, but it became obvious that she was not to be found anywhere on land that was in reach. And the feminine energy of the Lemurians would not be finding what they needed. So humans began to search elsewhere.

Then came the time of Abraham, Isaac, Jacob, and most importantly, his twelve children. They began to look outside themselves for answers to the questions that tormented them. In wanting something that they could not get on Earth, they created a space that was everything else that they could want. I believe that space has been called God. There was an existence of God in the previous cultures in Kenya and Italy but that existence was in danger of becoming extinct. During the time in Israel six thousand years ago the existence of God as previously known was becoming impossible to live with due to the lack of human nurturing necessary. So to make sure the existence known as God wasn't lost, the twelve tribes dedicated their lives to make sure that God was not lost from existence. God became something objective that could be cared for, before this the existence that is known as God had always been subjective. Today, for the most part, God is seen as objective but ideally God is subjective.

From this time around 4000 BC, the Second World moved southwest a little to Egypt. The year was about

2600 BC, and a boom of civilization was occurring. Under Pharaoh Djoser, his father and grandfather—not to mention his firstborn son and grandson and so on—there was an air of empowerment.

During this time, the civilized world was fed by a man named Imhotep, who was actually Pharaoh Djoser's younger brother. Imhotep cared for the people of Egypt by teaching and practicing healing on the people. To some, he is truly the first Western doctor in history. He also went above and beyond for the people by teaching and practicing alchemy. The alchemy that Imhotep practiced really had nothing to do with turning lead into gold, but was actually a method of healing the social issues that affected the culture on a daily basis. Maybe this high priest was akin to the modern-day psychologist or shaman. The alchemy was able to lighten up any heavy situation.

Once he had done the work for the people, they were happy to work for him and the pharaoh. He decided to do something for his family that had never done before. To the Egyptians death was felt to be as sacred as life, and the people of Egypt had lived such a wonderful life, Imhotep decided to celebrate the sacred nature of death by designing a stairway to the stars: the step pyramid called Saqqara. The pyramid was also a way to remember the feelings related to the death of a loved one.

About thirty-five hundred years ago, things began to ease up. At the time of Krishna, men and women alike began to find peace and pleasure in a freedom that had never been experienced. During this time in India, people were being receptive to the ideas of God and being emotionally expressive. The combination of the intellectual creation of God and the emotional desire to live in that world created a great home.

The mathematics of the Second World's presence in everyday life is quite easy to figure out. The Second World's effect on the inner world is 2/5, or 40%, which means that forty percent of our internal thoughts and feelings come from the Second World. The effect of the Second World on our everyday outer existence is 5/2, or 250%. At 250%, people are able to live subtly, or aloof. For those that aren't satisfied with living a subtle lifestyle, the people that live in the outer world of the Second World are usually very strong in character and have a very powerful presence.

To help yourself, what you will need to do is take that 40% of your internal life and the 250% of your outer life and combine them, so that they equal one, or in other words: Oneness. Now that you have divided the world to make it easier to understand and realize, it is time to put it back together, and it happens quite naturally: 2/5 x 5/2 = 10/10 or 1.

WORLD 3

World Three is a world that is honestly so simple that it is complex. In the Third World, approximately twenty-five hundred years ago, somewhere in the area of northern India, there was a young prince, or at least that is how the story goes. When he reached the age of puberty and had struggled with his primal tendencies for long enough, it was time for a new solution to an old problem. He wanted to leave his family and the world around him to follow his heart: to answer his call of nature.

He spent an amount of time that felt like years in quest of that which seemed to be leading him. On the quest he went through many hardships to get to where he had to go, and some of these experiences were learning how to live purely with nature again. He energetically became one with birds as they flew and with the trees. Once his guides could no longer help the young boy grow they parted ways, and the young man continued on. After the journey and all the new learning experiences, he finally found that part of nature that was calling him: his soul mate. This was the woman that he was married to and had about nine children with in the First World in Africa, and she was the missing piece to his heart for tens of thousands of years.

The two of them shared a limited amount of time together, mainly because the journey had changed the young prince into a learned young man. The time was so limited because of the lack of respect that his soul mate and her family showed him, for he had become a man who had left his family and home to satisfy his heart and soul, and all she and her family knew was how to treat people like children.

The two lovers did spend enough time together to unknowingly conceive a child. The young man did not know that his soul mate was pregnant, and her parents were being very mean to him every day. The young man could no longer live with her family and be true to himself, so he left. And his lover couldn't go with him. The young man was torn between his desires: the desire to stay and the desire to go. But from experience the young man knew what the right thing to do was, and that was to leave.

He spent another period of time walking, this time with the hopes to clear his mind out. One day it got to a point where he could no longer walk with a free mind and a free heart in any direction. So he just sat down and thought about what was going on in his life. He thought that, in a short period of time, he left his family and didn't want to return home. He left his soul mate and her family and would not return there due to the pain that she and her family were causing him. So he thought. Then he stopped to eat or sleep, and then he thought, never forgetting anyone or anything that was behind him.

Then there is a story that says that almost exactly nine months from the time he spent with his soul mate, during which he thought and thought and thought, she lived in enough pain to empathize with the young man. She gave birth to their daughter, and that moment broke the hearts and minds of all that were involved. The young man's heart and mind were broken open, and the emotion and new mindset created a space in time called Nirvana.

This is one possible story of how the beginning of the Third World came to be, and it is the one that I live by. I do believe the beginning of the Third World was when Siddhartha became the Buddha by attaining Nirvana.

Mathematically, 60%, or 3/5, of our inner world is affected by the Third World. People that are living in the inner world of the Third World are less concerned will material things. For these people, the value of peace and freedom are more than the value of a world surrounded by material things to keep you busy. These people are more content being than doing. There are some negative traits from the inner world of the Third World. Some of them are seen in behaviors that are considered obsessive-compulsive. From obsessive-compulsive traits that are socially accepted, you may find the root of actions that are considered greedy or addictive.

Our outer life is affected by 5/3, or 166.66%, of the Third World, and it shows itself in forms of out-of-control chemical attraction between people. The positive traits of the outer world of the Third World can be seen in people that are calm and composed in situations when others are panicking.

WORLD 4

The Fourth World began approximately two thousand years ago in Israel. A son in a family of six children was taught the Torah by his mother and learned to work with his hands with his father. One day around the age of a bar mitzvah, he got to speak with a bunch of rabbis in Jerusalem. He spoke with the rabbis and realized that he was different than them, more enlightened then them. They, the rabbis, and the boy were both Jewish, but it was as if they spoke a different language. The young man felt that his way of Judaism was more truthful than the Judaism that the rabbis lived by. He felt their way was more based on the miracles of Moses than on the Twelve Tribes of Israel. So the young man continued to practice the form of Judaism that felt most familiar to him.

After years of work away from the big city, the young man was in a way called to do God's work, and that led him back to Jerusalem. When he arrived in Jerusalem with his mother and brother, he was immediately validated by a well-known man of God, John the Baptist, who I believe also happened to be his uncle.

From there he began to the walk and do as his heart desired. He met friends along the way that chose to stay with him, along with his mother and brother. One of the people that approached him was a woman known as Mary Magdalene, also known as his soul mate. The one and only, from Africa in the First World and India in the Third World.

The young man traveled around teaching whoever desired to be taught or healed. Eventually the law caught up with him. With fear of losing their power, they interrogated him on his actions. He was unable to defend himself to their satisfaction, for they didn't really speak the same language. He was a man of God, and his interrogators were not.

He continued to live his creative lifestyle to his dying day, because it was the only way he knew how to live. While being tortured to death, unknowingly he was receiving a similar fate as the men on each side of him, his older and younger brothers of the First World, Italy, Egypt, and the Third World in India. And in a moment right before this young Jewish man's death, the Fourth World was born.

Mathematically, our Fourth World inner world is 4/5, or 80%, of our present inner world. For some people, living with 80% of their inner potential is good enough for them, but not for everyone. The Fourth World affects our outer world by 5/4, or 125%. Some people look upon the expressions that are 125% and incorrectly think that it is 100%. Because of this, they are extremely wrong about reality in the Fifth World time and time again. This mistake is the nature for a majority of occasions where people are 100% wrong and are clueless of what is right.

WORLD 5

The Fifth World is the world that we are currently living in. On December 21, 2012, the Fifth World became critical mass and mainstream. I do believe that some people have gotten glimpses of the new world over the recent past.

After the horrors of the Holocaust and what led up to it, people needed to believe in a better world. The baby boomer generation led the movement, as they lived their lives and raised their children. The assassination of John F. Kennedy may have been an event that made Americans cry out for answers to actions that seemed to be senseless. As the sixties slowly went by, the greatest leaders of the time were being killed, making all types of people ask larger questions about life. Since the forties and maybe before, some individual people have been awakened to the Fifth World.

I personally had the experience of the car's horn that awakened me to the Fifth World on approximately August 30, 1995. I have lived for seventeen plus years, working diligently on finding acceptance of my vision that has become the Fifth World.

It is a lifetime where we do have the choice to choose the lives that we want to live. If you choose to be ignorant, for the freedom that it gives you, then be ignorant and enjoy your life. If you choose to hold on to sad memories that you choose not to forget, then I hope that you live in peace with those memories. And if you choose to live a life of love, peace, and truth, I hope you have a smile on while you are doing it and a feeling of fulfillment every day.

The Fifth World mathematically is the constant. The effect of the Fifth World on the Fifth World's inner and outer worlds is 5/5, or 100%. Over the years, I hope it will be more possible to realize what it means to live in the Fifth World within this structure. The awakening is the first moment, and that is just the beginning of the work. And remember, this is a marathon not a sprint. So take your time and enjoy it.

In the Fifth World, you are given opportunities to live in different worlds and remain grounded in the Fifth World. There is a whole world of fascinating existences, from deep mystical worlds to worlds of higher intelligence that are here on earth to educate and entertain us. From them you can enrich and excite your life in the Fifth World. I also think that it would be polite to mention that I believe that the epicenter of Fifth World energy is located about twenty miles southeast of Four Corners. It is a National Park in New Mexico called Shiprock, and it is truly magnificent.

SEPARATED			BALANCED TOGETHER
Inner World		**Outer World**	
1/5 or 20%		5/1 or 500%	5/5 = 1
2/5 or 40%		5/2 or 250%	10/10 = 1
3/5 or 60%		5/3 or 166.66%	15/15 = 1
4/5 or 80%		5/4 or 125%	20/20 = 1
5/5 or 100%		5/5 or 100%	25/25 = 1
6/5 or 120%		5/6 or 83.33%	30/30 = 1
7/5 or 140%		5/7 or 71.42871%	35/35 = 1
8/5 or 160%		5/8 or 62.5%	40/40 = 1
9/5 or 180%		5/9 or 55.55%	45/45 = 1
10/5 or 200%		5/10 or 50%	50/50 = 1
11/5 or 220%		5/11 or 45.45%	55/55 = 1
12/5 or 240%		5/12 or 41.66%	60/60 = 1

WORLD 6

The Sixth World is the first world in this structure that is located in the future. I believe that the Sixth World will begin in approximately one hundred years and will be based in Israel. The Sixth World will be known as the time of the Jewish Messiah. In the Sixth World, soul mates will live together in relative love and peace, which is something that we have not had for a lifetime in the majority in seventy thousand years.

Also, the coming of the Jewish Messiah is said to be accompanied by peace for two thousand years, and I do believe that is true. But I am sad to say that there may still be fighting and issues and disagreements. The peace and love of the soul mates will last two thousand years until the next world, when truth will attempt to be the third part of that equation: love, peace, and truth. Peace is a state of being, and being at peace with the reality that there are people still fighting with each other may be the most peace that can be achieved. Either way, the acceptance of love and peace by the majority will be something that defines the Sixth World.

Mathematically, how the Sixth World affects the inner world of the Fifth World is 6/5, or 120%. I believe that this may lead some people to try too hard to fix everything now: people trying to fit 120% of reality into a box that only holds 100%.

To those that want to help and live in the Fifth World, there is a certain subdued, receptive nature that is very healthy. To those who want to live in the Sixth World and remain connected to the Fifth World, I recommend an unconditional acceptance of reality, and a keen wit that can differentiate good from bad and right from wrong. The inner part of the Sixth World is 120%, and in the Fifth World, anything over 110% is spiritual, or immaterial.

Worlds One through Twelve

The part of the Sixth World that affects our outer world is 5/6, or 83.33%. Therefore the truth is that you may want something like peace and love, but there isn't enough of it out there to make it substantial enough to build a life with. You will have enough of the outer Sixth World to survive and to maintain a quiet, private life but not enough to nurture a healthy public life.

WORLD 7

The Seventh World will be about two thousand years after the Sixth World, and it may take place somewhere around India or China. The Seventh World as a space in time is the same as Nirvana. The Seventh World, or Nirvana, is a lifestyle that is recognizable by the clarity of an enlightened mind. In Nirvana, the enlightened mind is able to think out the most logical and rational way of dealing with any personal issue, yours or theirs. I believe that when people say they have reached Nirvana, they are speaking of attaining the Seventh World in connection with the previous six worlds. In other words, the combination of Worlds One through Seven is, in my opinion, the lifestyle of Nirvana.

Since this structure is grounded in everyday reality, or the Fifth World, we are unable to live in Nirvana 100% of the time and remain in connection with the Fifth World. To explain this I use the simplicity of mathematics.

Mathematically, the Seventh World affects the outer world of the Fifth World 5/7, or 71.42871% repeating. This 71.42871% is a very pure and light-hearted percent of the Fifth World. In the Fifth World, anything under 80% is not considered material, or something of matter. You may find the outer part of the Seventh World in people that have chosen to make the material world secondary. Also, many great old Eastern sayings come from expressions from the outer world of the Seventh World.

The inner world of the Seventh World's effect on the Fifth World is 7/5, or 140%. In there, there is a large quantity of a peaceful lifestyle filled with enlightened thought, or for younger minds, it may be called daydreaming. For older minds, if may be described as the state you might be in when you are drunk or high. A more relaxed and less stressful existence awaits us in the Seventh World. Where Fifth World love becomes a second nature, Sixth World peace is the popular way, and enlightened truth is in abundance in the Seventh World.

WORLD 8

The Eighth World, I believe, will return back to the United States of America, where the energy of Shiprock will again be the focal point, or it may be Kenya for the second time or even somewhere in South America. I do not know for sure how far in the future this will be, but my best guess is that it will most likely be about four or five thousand years away from today.

The Eighth World will be a world of returning to nature. The Eighth World will be a time when people will, through their enlightened thought, think first of the land that takes care of us, and ourselves second. There may be reasons for taking care of the earth first, maybe because of all the destruction over the past thousands of years will have left the planet unbalanced. And this speaks of electromagnetic energies needing to be balanced for the health of the planet. With enlightened thought: if the land that you walk on is chemically unbalanced, then so too will be the people that walk on the land.

Mathematically, the Eighth World affects the outer world of the Fifth World 5/8, or 62.5%. This 62.5% is the part of us that truly cares about nature and all that is natural. It is the part of us that sees the beauty in a landscape, not as something that we can make a profit off of but as something that feeds our existence, and without it we will not exist.

The inner world of the Eighth World affects the Fifth World by 8/5, or 160%. The inner world of the Eighth World is comparable to the feeling of being closer to the earth that we live on, or home. It is a very powerful, deep feeling of belonging and comfort. This feeling is as it is because the person who is experiencing it is not seen as different from the land that they are feeling. They are one and the same with the land that they sleep on, eat on, sit on, work on, and live on. In the Eighth World we, as cultures will learn or remember what it is like to truly accept and be accepted by the living being called the planet Earth.

WORLD 9

The Ninth World is a world that can be defined by one word, Christlike. The Twelfth World, I believe will be in existence in about twenty thousand years from the present. As for the Ninth, Tenth, and Eleventh Worlds. I truly do not have an accurate enough timeline. The Eighth World will be in approximately four or five thousand years from now, and the Twelfth World will be about twenty thousand years from now. So the Ninth, Tenth, and Eleventh Worlds will be in existence sometime between five and twenty thousand years from now.

The Ninth World will possibly be located somewhere in Europe, or maybe Israel. It will be during the Ninth World that the science of resurrection will be validated and exemplified. The Ninth World will be the lifetime of the Second Coming of Christ. In the Ninth World, the soul of Christ will return to the planet Earth and so will the body of Christ, that being the definition of resurrection.

This being the Fifth World, I must put a disclaimer on this explanation with 55.55% of my Fifth World outer being. I am personally not sure that the Second Coming of Christ will have 100% the same body as the body he had two thousand years ago. I presently believe in resurrection as the scientific side to the art form of reincarnation.

The outer world of the Ninth World's effect on the Fifth World will be 5/9, or 55.55% repeating. This 55.55% is the part of us that passionately wants to do good and nice things. Also, the outer part of the Ninth World is seen in expressions of unexpected acts of kindness.

The inner part of the Ninth World's effect on the Fifth World is 9/5, or 180%. This 180% is best exemplified by the thing that we call our conscience, that little voice in our head that knows the right thing to do.

WORLD 10

After the Ninth World, there will be the Tenth World, which will be located, I believe, somewhere in the area of the Middle East. The location of the Tenth World will possibly be in Sumeria, the southern region of Iraq or Israel, Egypt, or maybe even Mecca.

The Tenth World will take the general politeness of the Ninth World and give confidence to people to truly be themselves. In today's world of the Fifth World, one can usually be themselves to the limit that is defined as superficial. But the Tenth World will offer people the ability to be themselves at a much deeper level of the soul. This, I believe, is part of the message of Muhammad the prophet that has come to be Allah. It is a world that is focused on the Self, in the Hindu sense of Atman.

The outer part of World Ten is 5/10, or 50%, of our Fifth World existence. This part of your outer world longs to be in connection with the deepest possible part of our soul and to connect and remained connected with others, along with the planet earth at that deep level.

The inner part of the Tenth World's effect on the Fifth World is 10/5, or 200%. This 200% simply wants to connect their true self with someone else to give themselves and the other the feeling of home—warm, safe, and familiar—and to create an existence in this inner world of the Tenth World that may be referred to as the existence called Allah.

WORLD 11

The Eleventh World will possibly be somewhere around India or Tibet, or maybe even in California. It is a world that is best defined as the passive expression of humanity. This Eastern philosophical world, I believe, will allow the passive side of our behaviors to rule our lifestyle in the Eleventh World.

The Eleventh World will be the expressions of a repressed lifestyle that was created by Krishna. When Krishna lived his life in the Second World, his primary way of life was not accepted by his parents, and therefore society. Krishna was one of at least six children, and his father Brahma had more public influence on how people would live their lives. As Krishna grew, he chose to hide his way of life for the most part. He did not hide the majority of himself from some of his siblings and his wife and children. Krishna's way of life was so advanced that it is not until the Eleventh World that his creations come to maturation and acceptance.

Being passive and receptive are the keys to existence in the Eleventh World. If you want an answer to a question, just be receptive to the answer and you will receive it. If you are sick and you want to be healed, just be receptive and accept the cure to your illness that will find you. And if you want to be loved, just open up and receive the love that will come to you.

The outer world of the Eleventh World's effect on the Fifth World is 5/11, or 45.45%. The outer world of the Eleventh World in the Fifth World can be seen in people that appear to have everything but aren't doing anything with it. In the outer part of the Eleventh World in the Fifth World, you need to nurture your potential and make the best of what you can with it.

The inner world of the Eleventh World's effect on the Fifth World is 11/5, or 220%. This 220% can be difficult to comprehend. An example of an action that is 220% is when someone says or does something that seems to come out of nowhere and it is the perfect solution, like inspiration or aspiration. A Fifth World existence in the inner world of the Eleventh World can be explained as subtle. Subtle sounds have meaning: subtle senses like the feelings of the wind can subtly awaken your consciousness. Sensitivity and awareness of these subtleties are good examples of existence in the inner world of the Eleventh World.

WORLD 12

I have chosen the Twelfth World as the last world of this structure for good reason. It is always nice to end things on a good note. Besides, I believe that it is the last world that is functional in this structure. The world does not end at the end of the Twelfth World. It is just that as we are living in the Fifth World, the Twelfth World is the last world of substance, of matter, and therefore is the last world that is able to be used consistently and functionally in the Fifth World.

The Twelfth World is a world in which familial love will rule. There will be so much love in the Twelfth World that everyone who wants and is open to familial love will have as much as they can handle. The basis for the Twelfth World is the Twelve Tribes of Israel.

During the time of the Twelve Tribes of Israel, 4000 BC, everyone was willing to live and die for each other. It was when people cared about each other so much that there was little else to care about. In an ideal reality, is there anything else to care about besides each other? By this time, the Eighth World had already taught us how to care for the planet. So in the Twelfth World, we have all the time in the world to care for each other.

The outer world of the Twelfth World's effect on the Fifth World is 5/12, or 41.66%. This can be seen in a child that just wants to love his/her mom or dad endlessly, or in siblings that just want to play together until it is too dark to see since the sun had gone down.

The inner world of the Twelfth World's effect on the Fifth World is 12/5, or 240%. The 240% of the Twelfth inner world on the Fifth World is heard in the expressions of the eternal optimist, and even more in the true idealist.

As you follow the worlds from the First to the Twelfth, it is possible to find yourself, or aspects of your personality, in each individual world. Each world may seem objective, but they are attainable by anyone who desires. And once attained, they become the subject of your life.

Once you find yourself in one of the twelve worlds, the goal is to accept your connection to the inner world and its characteristics, and the outer world and its characteristics of each world. Then once you have accepted both your inner world and outer world in any given world, you move on to combine the inner world and the outer world into one complete, balanced world. There are twenty-four separated worlds that can be uniquely brought together to create twelve individual worlds. Once each of the twelve worlds are balanced and unified, then the next step in the Worlds One through Twelve can be taken.

The next step is to combine the individual worlds into one whole unit of Worlds One through Twelve. It may be easier to combine the Fifth and the Fourth Worlds at first, to see how it works, and what you may find is over two thousand years of logic, mystery, and conflict. It is most likely easiest to combine the Fifth World with the Fourth World, because of all the twelve worlds, most people can comfortably relate to experiences in the Fifth and the

Fourth Worlds. Once you have found oneness with the Fifth World and oneness with the Fourth World separately, then you attempt to combine the oneness of the Fifth World and the oneness of the Fourth World into the oneness of the Fifth and Fourth Worlds combined. And it goes from there.

From here you may want to bring in the balancing love and peace of the Sixth World. After the Sixth World, you may want to familiarize yourself with the Third World, to give yourself the substance of a foreign past. After finding the future in the Sixth World to be pleasant and liberating, the experiencer might continue on to the Seventh and Eighth Worlds. Once getting to the Eighth World, you may need to experience more times when the earth wasn't in such a fragile state. By going back to the Second World, you can replenish your soul with great diversity and choice. From there you will have the energy and desire to go further into the Ninth and then the Tenth World. Time will seem to slow down as one will feel the feeling of being stuck in a room with no floor or ceiling.

Worlds One through Twelve

This is the Worlds Two through Ten, and when that happens, you will begin your journey downward. The nature of the Tenth World is to set out for that of most value. You will break through the Second World to the roots that are the First World. From there you will begin your last ascension in the structure of the Worlds One through Twelve. You will let go of the Tenth World and go to the Eleventh. From there you will make your final transition to the Twelfth World.

I personally have not gotten bored yet with the Worlds One through Twelve. Each time I journey through this structure, I find something new and exciting. Obviously, after studying the inner and outer parts of each world, you are free to go through this structure however you please. I was just showing an example of how I would go through them.

The final goal is to have Worlds One through Twelve as one balanced entity of space and time. The structure is nearly one hundred thousand years of metaphysical knowledge and emotion: some that has already happened, some that will happen, and all that is happening right now in the Fifth World.

PART V

REINCARNATION

REINCARNATION

Reincarnation is the soul's rebirth into a new body. I believe that the act of reincarnation is a process that allows the soul of a human being to be reborn into a more evolved physical body. I also believe that animals reincarnate but into more evolved physical bodies of the same animals. The reasoning for reincarnation being an act that coexists with evolution is simply factual due to chronology. The world continues to evolve. Even though there may be times of apparent devolution on some level, the world continues to evolve, or change.

You can find theories of reincarnation in almost every religion. I find the Hindu definition to be the purest. The Hindu definition of reincarnation states that one person's soul embodies itself in the human form, and it is the same soul that passes from lifetime to lifetime. This lifetime is a very special one because I believe that everyone on this planet has been reincarnated. Or in other words, every person in existence has had a past life on this planet.

There are many, if not all, of the famous people of the past that I am aware of alive right now in the present or recently deceased. Besides all of the famous people, not to minimize their importance in any way, there are billions of people that have been reincarnated for the sole, or soul, purpose of restoring their native cultures. These native cultures are expressions of the land and expressions of the past actions, issues, or karma. The native incarnations deal with whatever is impeding the healthy growth of their culture. These people have been reincarnated in order to nurture the truth and purity of their land. Sadly, in current times it has become difficult for the land to nurture itself within the reality of the world of industry.

I know from my ability to read people's past lives, which is one of the most outstanding gifts that I received on that day in New Orleans, that I have had the pleasure of knowing some of the greatest people either face-to-face or over some form of media. To list a few: Cleopatra is alive today as is Joan of Arc; Babe Ruth and Lou Gehrig are alive today along with Humphrey Bogart and James Dean; Shakespeare is alive and well along with Dante and Edgar Allan Poe; J.P. Morgan, Andrew Mellon and Cornelius Vanderbilt are alive and well; Martin Luther King is alive today along with Mahatma Gandhi and Martin Luther; Confucius, Lao-Tzu and Chang-Tzu are alive along with Nostradamus and Edgar Cayce; the Apostles James, Thomas, and Andrew are alive along with the other nine apostles and the disciples of the Buddha; Abraham, Sarah, Isaac, Rebecca, Esau, and Jacob are alive; John F. and Robert Kennedy are alive along with Jefferson, Teddy and Franklin Roosevelt, and just about every other ex-president of the United States of America; Queen Elizabeth I, Queen Victoria and even Princess Diana are alive today; Jerry Garcia is alive today along with Bob Marley, John Lennon, and Elvis Presley; Pythagoras, Hippocrates, Charles Darwin, and Pavlov are alive along with Christopher Columbus, Magellan, and Ponce de Leon; Socrates, Aristotle, Spinoza and Nietzsche are alive along with Freud and Jung; Benjamin Franklin, Edison, Newton, and Einstein are alive today along with Madame Marie Curie; Michelangelo, Raphael, and da Vinci are alive today along with Monet and Van Gogh; and these are just a fraction of the famous reincarnations that I know of. And I have chosen to leave out the infamous ones.

To bring some more clarity to the first part of this book, I will tell you the past lives of some of the characters with hopes of easing the hard work that I have with them. First, I will list the past lives of Jessica. She is on her seventh lifetime, which is tied for second most. My mother, father, older and younger brothers are on their seventh lives too. Jessica was my sister in Africa, Italy, Egypt, my second life in India, two thousand years ago in Israel, and she was also Queen Elizabeth I in her most recent past life.

My ex-girlfriend Ali was my wife in Africa, the mother of my child in my second life in India, and Mary Magdalene. My ex-roommate Matt has a controversial list of past lives. He was my and Ali's first child in Africa, and then he was

Leah's third son in Israel six thousand years ago. Jacob had two children with Rachel, the oldest being Joseph. Then Jacob had ten children with Leah. I was the first child of Jacob and Leah's, and Matt was the third. So this means that in one life he was my son, and in another he was my younger brother. I don't think that either of us have come to terms with this dynamic. After that life he was President Thomas Jefferson. Also the Hopi medicine man, Emery, was, I believe, John Emory. John Emory was the man that Emory University was named for.

My friends Alex, Kate, and Brad are a bit more controversial. I believe that Brad was my grandfather's brother in Africa and Herod the Great two thousand years ago. Alex was my grandson is Africa, then he was Alexander the Great, then he was Herod Antipas, and his most recent past life was Ron "Pigpen" McKernan, one of the founding members of the Grateful Dead. Kate was, is, and always will be Alex's soul mate, just as Ali is mine. Kate and Alex were together in Africa and their children were my great-grandchildren, and then Kate's next life was a man named Pontius Pilate. Kate's most recent past life was Henri Matisse.

The 5th World

Also for your information, my yoga instructor was my wife in a past life, and her daughter was our daughter in that past life. And the two police officers that beat me up in the New Orleans jail were actually disciples of the Buddha in their past lives. From here I will list my past lives.

I have reincarnated seven times, which means that I am on my eighth life. I spent my first lifetime in eastern Africa during the First World. I spent my second lifetime in Italy, living in Atlantis. My third lifetime was in Israel, as one of the Twelve Tribes of Israel. In that life my name was Judah. I lived my third reincarnated life, or fourth life, in Egypt as the pharaoh's brother Imhotep. I lived my fifth life in India, possibly as the one who realized the existence of reincarnation as Krishna. I lived my sixth life somewhere in northern India as Siddhartha, and later as the Buddha. I lived my sixth reincarnation, or seventh lifetime, in Israel as a young Jewish man that was killed on a cross, and my name was Yahshua, which means salvation in Hebrew, or by my better known name of Jesus.

And in this incarnation, my name is Michael Rotman. I am enjoying my existence as a mystic to the best of my abilities. I consider the United States of America to be my home, especially the Main Line outside of Philadelphia, New Orleans, and Northern Arizona.

I had a vision, and I believe that my life can improve by incorporating more of my vision into my everyday life. I believe that this book can have a positive influence on other peoples' lives. The other reason for writing this book is so I don't have to tell the same stories from scratch to each person that I meet, as I did for seventeen years.

In this life I am limited as to what I can do by society and my health, and I have accepted that. Within my limits, I hope to have a good, happy, healthy, and full life. And I hope my life affects as many other people's lives as possible.

Thank You

Made in the USA
Middletown, DE
23 July 2021